DEDICATION

This resource book is lovingly dedicated to the pastoral team, catechumens, and candidates of Our Lady of the Valley Parish in Canoga Park, California, from 1983 to 1988. It was they who first called me forth as a minister of Christian initiation. They challenged me, believed in me, and humbled me by their faith and commitment. Because of them I fell in love with the ministry of Christian initiation. Because of them, I celebrate my own baptism with gratitude and awe.

ENTER THE ROSE

*Retreats for Unfolding the Mysteries of Faith
with Catechumens, Candidates, and All Believers*

MIRIAM MALONE, SNJM

017289

WORLD LIBRARY PUBLICATIONS
the music and liturgy division of J. S. Paluch Company, Inc.
3708 River Road, Suite 400, Franklin Park, Illinois 60131-2158
800 566-6150 www.wlpmusic.com

ENTER THE ROSE

WLP 017289

ISBN
1-58459-147-1

Author: Miriam Malone, SNJM
Artwork and Graphics: Jean Morningstar, SNJM
Music Arrangements for Audio CD: Jerry Galipeau
Editor: Jerry Galipeau
Copy Editor: Marcia T. Lucey
Design: Tejal Patel

Enter the Rose: Retreats for Unfolding the Mysteries of Faith with Catechumens, Candidates, and All Believers © 2004, World Library Publications, the music and liturgy division of J. S. Paluch Company, Inc., 3708 River Road, Suite 400, Franklin Park, Illinois 60131-2158.

Scripture quotations are from the New Revised Standard Version of the Bible, Copyright © 1989 by the Division of Christian Education of the National Council of the Churches of Christ in the USA.

Excerpts from the *Rite of Christian Initiation of Adults* © 1985, International Committee on English in the Liturgy, Inc. All rights reserved. Used with permission.

This work was originally published in 2002 by the Sisters of the Holy Names under the title *Enter the Rose: Unfolding the Mysteries of Faith*.

All rights reserved under United States copyright law. The original purchaser is authorized to duplicate the journals contained in this work and on the accompanying CD-ROM free of charge for any one-time use solely by his/her own parish. Reproduction in any other format or frequency is expressly prohibited without the written permission of the copyright holder. Removal of the copyright notice is prohibited. No other part of this book may be reproduced or transmitted in any form or by any means, mechanical, photographic, or electronic, including taping, recording, photocopying, or any information storage and retrieval system, without the written permission of the appropriate copyright owner.

Contents

Foreword vi
Acknowledgments viii
About the Title, Artist, Audio CD, CD-ROM,
    and SNJM FIRE for Ministry .... ix–xi
Music Suggestions xii
Index of Retreat Journals xiv
Introduction 1

Chapter 1: Foundations and Principles of Initiation 3

Chapter 2: The Period of Evangelization and Precatechumenate (Inquiry) 11
    Advent Twilight Retreat for Inquirers 13
    Lenten Twilight Retreat for Inquirers 18
    Discernment Retreat Prior to the Rite of Acceptance
        into the Order of Catechumens 22

Chapter 3: Catechumenate 31
    Twilight Retreat: The Rites Belonging to the Period of the Catechumenate 33
    Marian Retreat for the Catechumenate 38
    Discernment Retreat for the Rite of Election 45

Chapter 4: Candidates for Full Initiation 55
    Lenten Retreat for Candidates 57
    Retreat with the Woman at the Well 63

Chapter 5: Purification and Enlightenment 71
    Twilight Retreat: The First Scrutiny 73
    Twilight Retreat: The Second Scrutiny 78
    Holy Saturday Retreat and Preparation Rites 82

Chapter 6: Mystagogy 89
    Advent Retreat for the Fully Initiated 91
    Pentecost Anniversary Retreat for the Fully Initiated 101

FOREWORD

Enter the Rose: What a passionate title for this marvelous resource! *The Rite of Christian Initiation of Adults*, declared by the Bishops of the United States to be the normative process by which adults are initiated into the Roman Catholic Church, states that conversion is at the heart of the process. Such conversion is invited and prompted by God, and with the help of the Holy Spirit, a person freely responds. In Chapter One of *Enter the Rose*, Miriam Malone succinctly states the foundations and principles for the Rite of Christian Initiation. It would behoove a catechumenal team to read and ponder carefully the assumptions she offers as basic to the initiation process. Often team members can become so focused on the immediate needs of those in the process that they lose their sense of direction: the goal of the initiation process is discipleship and the mission of Jesus Christ. Sometimes a team can become so involved in the journey with those who are seeking the sacraments of initiation that they may forget who is in charge and who initiates—God. Or the team can lose sight of the fact that initiation is the responsibility of all the baptized, and that one of the roles of the team is to help the baptized—the community—to perform its ministry. Chapter One clearly reminds the team of its role. This chapter alone makes this resource a very valuable one.

Enter the Rose is a unique resource for the catechumenal team. It provides for its users a variety of retreat opportunities for the various stages of the initiation process. The settings, processes, and possibilities for gathering persons who are on the journey of initiation into the Catholic Church are not difficult to implement. A novice on the team would find it easy to facilitate such a retreat. Miriam has given detailed information for the facilitator. More experienced team members will find great flexibility in these outlines and will be able to use the format to its greatest potential to engage the retreatants at various stages of their journey of faith.

Each retreat has four components: the context, word of God, sacred space, and living rite. Each of these basic elements, presented in a variety of ways, provides the facilitator with concrete ways of facilitating a retreat, whether it is for a few hours or an extended period of time. An additional bonus of this resource is the audio CD that includes formation guidance for the facilitator. The retreats prepare the catechumens for particular rites of the initiation process: acceptance, election, scrutiny, and initiation. They also incorporate the minor rites of the process. Each plan includes a ritual that celebrates the focus of the retreat. Following solid adult education principles, *Enter the Rose* engages the participants through quiet time, journal questions, one-on-one sharing, input, and ritual action.

A unique feature of *Enter the Rose* is the retreat offerings it provides for candidates—those who are already one with us through baptism and who seek communion with us—or for those who are seeking to complete their initiation through the celebration of confirmation and eucharist. Often these candidates are included in the initiation activities as if they were not baptized. These retreat offerings highlight the status of candidates who are already baptized into the family of God. They are an excellent means of preparation for the candidate as he or she is readied for reception into full communion.

Other features of *Enter the Rose* are retreats for the neophytes, those who are in the final period of the initiation process, or mystagogy. Mystagogy is often the team's greatest challenge. Miriam Malone offers the team two marvelous opportunities to gather with the neophytes. These retreats would capture the imagination of the neophytes and propel them forward with renewed energy and commitment to be faithful disciples of Jesus Christ.

Enter the Rose need not be limited to use with those in the initiation process. What Miriam Malone has written is a valuable tool that could easily be adapted to a variety of groups such as a small Christian community, a faith sharing group, a women's group, a men's group, a neighborhood group, etc. Its possibilities are unlimited. The four components become a model for future retreats. The facilitator could adapt these retreats to any number of other gatherings of people who want to reflect on their journey of faith.

Throughout the book, *Enter the Rose* invites its user to contemplate the beauty and imagery of a rose. What a joy to have such a treasure at our fingertips. At last, a resource that helps the team to focus on the spiritual journey of adults, a journey that varies with the many circumstances of life. It is truly a gift! You will not be disappointed. *Enter the Rose* and savor the beauty of God's creation.

Gael Gensler, OSF

Gael Gensler, a Clinton, Iowa Franciscan, is presently the pastoral associate at Julie Billiart Parish in Tinley Park, Illinois. She has been involved in adult and children's initiation for twenty years. Gael has served as Director of Institutes and is a team member of the North American Forum on the Catechumenate. She has written extensively on the topic of initiation, including materials for Resources for Christian Living's Foundations in Faith *series, Resource Publications of San Jose, California and other publications. She is a frequent presenter on a variety of initiation topics.*

ACKNOWLEDGMENTS

With gratitude, I acknowledge the many people who supported me and helped to make the dream of this project come true.

Thank you, my Sisters of the Holy Names, who encouraged me to pursue the dream and to take the time to bring this project to birth.

Thank you, Jean Morningstar, SNJM, for your wonderful gift of art, for your willingness to collaborate on this project, for bringing the concepts and principles of initiation to life in graphic form.

Thank you, Mary Ann Connell, SNJM, for bringing the perspectives of theologian and practitioner to each draft, and for your constructive and encouraging critique.

Thank you, Gael Gensler, OSF, for your support, and especially for the time you spent reading through the project and writing the Foreword.

Thank you, Jerry Galipeau, for your interest in the project, for your generous encouragement, for your editorial skill, and for sharing your wonderful, artistic gift of music.

Thank you, Scott Barta of Pacific Soundcraft, for your professionalism, patience, and skill in engineering the audio CD.

Thank you, my friends, and especially my good neighbor Martha Rolley, SNJM, and Mary Ambrose Devereux, SNJM, who celebrated with me in times of creativity and completion, and believed in me and prodded me on in times of doubt, discouragement, and writer's block.

Thank you, my wonderful Mom and Dad, and all my family, for your support and encouragement and for your faith in me and in my work.

Thank you, Church of Los Angeles, from whom I learned the challenges of large parishes, many cultures, diverse languages, economic and educational inequities, and with whom I learned to know and love the Rite of Christian Initiation of Adults.

Thank you, Church of Juneau, Alaska, from whom I learned the power of two or three gathered in faith, the meaning of Church as People of God, and the privileges and responsibilities of the priesthood of the baptized.

Thank you to the many women and men who have blessed my life, who continue to bring to birth a new Church, and whose loving critique and courageous fidelity inspire me with hope.

THE TITLE

The phrase "Enter the Rose" was created by Noel Girard, SNJM. Noel was part of a planning group for a marvelous gathering of Sisters of the Holy Names of Jesus and Mary. The event called us to gather around our common mission to be gospel women inspired by the vision of Blessed Marie Rose Durocher, our foundress. We did this in the context of storytelling, reflection, creative expression, and inspiring ritual. Although "Enter the Rose" took place a number of years ago, its spirit lives on in each participant.

The spirit that characterized the gathering is the spirit that inspired this project. I am grateful to Noel for allowing us to use her creative title as the title of this project.

Marie Rose Durocher, a foundress of the Sisters of the Holy Names, shared with a small group of women her dream of working for the full human development of each person through education in the faith. Together, they followed that dream. Today, what a few visionary and courageous women began in a single room in the small village of Longueuil in Canada, has become an international congregation of Sisters and Associates serving in a variety of ministries throughout Canada, the United States, Lesotho, Brazil, Haiti, and Peru. Inspired by their dream, I am deeply grateful to participate in their mission by sharing this dream: *Enter the Rose: Unfolding the Mysteries of Faith*.

"The Sisters of the Holy Names are a community of women religious consecrated to God in the Names of Jesus and Mary, who desire to proclaim by our lives the primacy of the love of God. Moved by an active love we collaborate in the Church's mission of education with emphasis on education in the faith and with a special concern for the poor and disadvantaged" (*Constitutions of the Sisters of the Holy Names of Jesus and Mary*).

— *Miriam Malone, SNJM*

About the Artist

Jean Morningstar, SNJM, holds a master's degree in design from San Jose State University and a certificate from the Institute of Culture and Creation Spirituality at Holy Names College in Oakland. She taught elementary school for ten years and then spent twenty-one years as an instructor in art and photography on the secondary level. In 1984 she left formal education so that she could use her art to reach a wider audience. Sister Jean founded *Holy Names Graphics* in 1983. Since that time she has produced two lines of greeting cards, and 6 CDs of her original graphics, along with numerous logos, newsletters, and other graphic designs. Visit her Web site at www.holynamesgraphics.com.

About the Audio CD

The audio CD will guide you through the written materials. In the first two tracks you will be introduced to the contents of *Enter the Rose* and reminded of some basic principles of liturgical prayer and liturgical catechesis. Next are some suggestions for presiding at liturgical prayer; there are certain skills that will enhance the retreat experience if you become familiar with them and comfortable in your role as a presider.

In the remaining tracks, you will hear brief reflections, accompanied by Jerry Galipeau's music, focused on the stages of the initiation process, with introductions to each retreat, and a description of the content and some suggestions for implementation.

Track 1 *For Martha* **Reflection:** *Enter the Rose*
Track 2 **Introduction**
Track 3 **Overview, Attitudes, and Aptitudes**
Track 4 *Veni Sancte Spiritus* **Reflection:** *Enter the Rose*
Track 5 **The Precatechumenate**
Track 6 *Amazing Grace* **Reflection:** *Enter the Rose*
Track 7 **The Catechumenate**
Track 8 *Shaker Song* **Reflection:** *Enter the Rose*
Track 9 **Candidates**
Track 10 *Shall We Gather* **Reflection:** *Enter the Rose*
Track 11 **Purification and Enlightenment**
Track 12 *Alleluia, Sing to Jesus* **Reflection:** *Enter the Rose*
Track 13 **Mystagogy and Beyond**
Track 14 *For Martha* **Reflection:** *Enter the Rose*

About the CD ROM

The CD ROM contains the journals for all of the retreats. In order to view and print them, you must have Adobe Acrobat Reader on your computer.

About SNJM FIRE for Ministry

In-service formation sessions and support for implementing *Enter the Rose* are available through SNJM FIRE for Ministry.

Modules include:

- Resource Introduction and Overview
- Principles, Attitudes, and Aptitudes
- The Art of Liturgical Catechesis
- Creating Sacred Space
- Presiding Skills for Catechists and Retreat Leaders
- Discernment for Christian Initiation
- Implementing the Rite of Christian Initiation of Adults

To schedule your in-service workshop or retreat, contact:

SNJM FIRE for Ministry
www.snjmfire.com

SNJM FIRE for Ministry, a collaborative consulting group of Sisters of the Holy Names of Jesus and Mary, was formed to respond to a need for quality professional pastoral services within parishes, (arch)dioceses, schools, and religious congregations. SNJM FIRE personnel are qualified, experienced, expert ministers committed to excellence in education and the full development of the human person.

SNJM FIRE for Ministry personnel are available on an hourly, daily, weekly, or monthly basis depending on the needs of the sponsoring group.

MUSIC SUGGESTIONS FOR THE RETREATS

The following suggestions include the name of the publisher of the particular piece of music. Where no publisher is indicated, the piece is either in the public domain (not copyrighted) or can be found in most parish worship resources. Permission must be obtained from the copyright holder for the reproduction of any copyrighted piece of music.

WLP
WORLD LIBRARY PUBLICATIONS
3708 River Road, Suite 400
Franklin Park, IL 60131-2158
1 800 566-6150
www.wlpmusic.com

GIA
GIA PUBLICATIONS
7404 South Mason Avenue
Chicago, IL 60638
1 800 GIA-1358 (442-1358)
www.giamusic.com

OCP
OREGON CATHOLIC PRESS
5536 N.E. Hassalo
Portland, OR 97213
1 800 LITURGY (548-8749)
www.ocp.org

ADVENT TWILIGHT RETREAT FOR INQUIRERS
Come, Emmanuel (WLP)
Come, Light of the World (WLP)
The Hail Mary (WLP)
Look to the One (WLP)
Lead Us to Your Light (GIA)
My Soul in Stillness Waits (GIA)
Take, O Take Me as I Am (GIA)
Waiting in Silence (OCP)
Patience, People (OCP)
Ready the Way (OCP)

LENTEN TWILIGHT RETREAT FOR INQUIRERS
Grant to Us, O Lord (WLP)
From Ashes to the Living Font (WLP)
Strength for the Journey (WLP)
Hold Us in Your Mercy (GIA)
Deep Within (GIA)
Take, O Take Me as I Am (GIA)
Here I Am, Lord (OCP)
Lead Me, Guide Me

DISCERNMENT RETREAT PRIOR TO THE RITE OF ACCEPTANCE INTO THE ORDER OF CATECHUMENS
You Chosen Ones (WLP)
Set Your Heart on the Higher Gifts (WLP)
Take, O Take Me as I Am (GIA)
Who Calls You By Name (GIA)
Open My Eyes (OCP)
God Has Chosen Me (OCP)
Pescador de Hombres/Lord, You Have Come (OCP)
The Servant Song
Lead Me, Guide Me
I Want to Walk As a Child of the Light

TWILIGHT RETREAT: THE RITES BELONGING TO THE PERIOD OF THE CATECHUMENATE
Keep in Mind (WLP)
Come, All You Blessed Ones (WLP)
Healer of Our Every Ill (GIA)
O Lord, Hear My Prayer (GIA)
You Are the Healing (OCP)
Peace Is Flowing Like a River
Christ Be beside Me
Precious Lord, Take My Hand

MARIAN RETREAT FOR THE CATECHUMENATE
O Mary of Promise (WLP)
The Hail Mary (WLP)
Sing "Ave!" (WLP)
Ave Maria (GIA)
Hail Mary: Gentle Woman (OCP)
Hail, Holy Queen Enthroned Above
Immaculate Mary

DISCERNMENT RETREAT FOR THE RITE OF ELECTION
You Chosen Ones (WLP)
My Soul Is Longing (WLP)
All Will Be Well (WLP)
Now We Remain (GIA)
You Are Mine (GIA)
The Summons (GIA)
God Has Chosen Me (OCP)
I Will Choose Christ (OCP)
Now Is the Time (OCP)
I Heard the Voice of Jesus Say

LENTEN RETREAT FOR CANDIDATES
Gathered As One (WLP)
All Will Be Well (WLP)
My Soul Is Longing (WLP)
You Are Mine (GIA)
Take, O Take Me As I Am (GIA)
The Summons (GIA)
Gather Your People (OCP)
O God, You Search Me (OCP)
Center of My Life (OCP)
How Can I Keep From Singing

RETREAT WITH THE WOMAN AT THE WELL
Send Us Flowing Water (WLP)
Waters of Life (WLP)
O Healing River (GIA)
Change Our Hearts (GIA)
Flow, River, Flow (OCP)
Rain Down (OCP)
I Heard the Voice of Jesus Say

TWILIGHT RETREAT: THE FIRST SCRUTINY
Send Us Flowing Water (WLP)
O Healing River (GIA)
Change Our Hearts (GIA)
Flow, River, Flow (OCP)
Rain Down (OCP)
I Heard the Voice of Jesus Say

TWILIGHT RETREAT: THE SECOND SCRUTINY
In the Light (WLP)
I Want to Walk As a Child of the Light
Amazing Grace
We Are the Light of the World

HOLY SATURDAY RETREAT AND PREPARATION RITES
Here I Am, Lord (WLP, OCP)
You Chosen Ones (WLP)
You Are the Light of the World (WLP)
Who Calls You by Name (GIA)
Open My Eyes (OCP)
Servant Song (OCP)
This Day God Gives Me
The Church's One Foundation

ADVENT RETREAT FOR THE FULLY INITIATED
You Are the Light of the World (WLP)
On That Holy Mountain (WLP)
Christ, Be Our Light (OCP)
I Am the Light of the World (OCP)
I Want to Walk As a Child of the Light
O Come, O Come, Emmanuel
O Lord of Light

PENTECOST ANNIVERSARY RETREAT FOR THE FULLY INITIATED
Come, Holy Spirit, On Us Shine (WLP)
May You Cling to Wisdom (WLP)
The Spirit of God (WLP)
Spirit Blowing Through Creation (GIA)
Sweet, Sweet Spirit
O Breathe on Me, O Breath of God
O Holy Spirit, by Whose Breath
Come, Holy Ghost

INDEX OF RETREAT JOURNALS

This index will assist in locating the appropriate retreat journal for each of the retreats in *Enter the Rose*. The journals can be found on the accompanying CD ROM. The name of the file appears in brackets below.

The files have been designed to print in an order that will make duplication as simple as possible. The pages will not print in sequential order, but in an order that will assist you in photocopying the journals in a quick and easy manner. Once the pages of a file are printed, they should be placed in a photocopier in the exact order and paper orientation in which they were printed. Simply set the photocopier to print two-sided copies and sort the pages. The pages for the journals will print in exactly the right order. Once printed, the pages can be folded and stapled. Check the page numbers at the bottom of each page as a final check for accuracy.

Please note: "Holy Saturday Retreat and Preparation Rites" does not use a journal.

ADVENT TWILIGHT RETREAT FOR INQUIRERS
[Retreat01]

DISCERNMENT RETREAT PRIOR TO THE RITE OF ACCEPTANCE INTO THE ORDER OF CATECHUMENS
[Retreat03]

LENTEN TWILIGHT RETREAT FOR INQUIRERS
[Retreat02]

TWILIGHT RETREAT: THE RITES BELONGING TO THE PERIOD OF THE CATECHUMENATE
[Retreat04]

Marian Retreat for the Catechumenate
[Retreat05]

Discernment Retreat for the Rite of Election
[Retreat06]

Lenten Retreat for Candidates
[Retreat07]

Retreat with the Woman at the Well
[Retreat08]

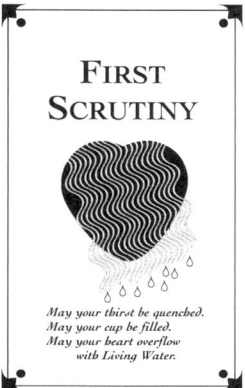

Twilight Retreat: The First Scrutiny
[Retreat09]

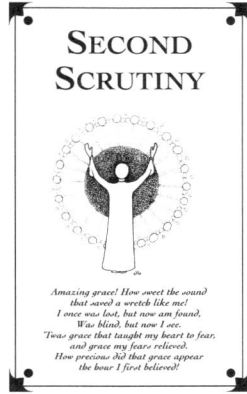

Twilight Retreat: The Second Scrutiny
[Retreat10]

Advent Retreat for the Fully Initiated
[Retreat11]

Pentecost Anniversary Retreat for the Fully Initiated
[Retreat12]

INTRODUCTION

The *Rite of Christian Initiation of Adults* is a journey of faith. It is an individual process of "unfolding" that is as unique as each of the persons who "consciously and freely seek the living God and enter the way of faith and conversion as the Holy Spirit opens their hearts" (¶1 RCIA). It is a gradual process of unfolding the mysteries of faith, which "takes place within the community of the faithful" who, by journeying with the catechumens and candidates, also renew their own conversion (¶4 RCIA). The image of the rose speaks to this magnificent journey of a lifetime.

Enter the Rose

It takes time to tend the rose.
Each rose has its own particular needs and growth patterns.
Tending the rose calls for patience and trust.
The beauty within is gradually revealed as the rose unfolds, each new layer
adding depth, color, fragrance, and promise of yet more wonder within.
It struggles splendidly toward its dying, its seed time.
The rose will not be forced; it answers to neither calendar nor deadline.
It follows the seasons inherent in its being and blooms in its own time.
It is sensitive to its surroundings,
    responsive to a healthy and nurturing environment,
while standing on its own and testifying to its uniqueness
    simply by being what it is.
It adds to the beauty of the garden, in harmony with the shapes, sizes, colors,
and fragrances of the other flowers.
And in the end, after the fullness of its bloom, it dies.
The wind blows, blessing the earth with seeds
    holding the memory of the rose
and the promise of a new life and beauty to come.

The minister of initiation is called to live the metaphor with each catechumen and candidate, in small rural communities and in parishes with large groups and a variety of cultures. The mandate of the minister of initiation is to provide for a "spiritual journey of adults that varies according to the many forms of God's grace, the free cooperation of the individuals, the action of the Church, and the circumstances of time and place" (¶5 RCIA). Is it possible, realistic, manageable?

The answer is, "yes!" It is the purpose of this book to provide practical support for that "yes!"

Chapter 1
Foundations and Principles of Initiation

ASSUMPTIONS

The purpose of this book is to provide ministers of initiation—catechists, directors, sponsors, and liturgical ministers—with resources to facilitate a variety of reflection and retreat experiences throughout the process of initiation. "Catechists, who have an important office for the progress of the catechumens and for the growth of the community, should, whenever possible, have an active part in the rites. . . . They may perform the minor exorcisms and blessings contained in the ritual. When they are teaching, catechists should see that their instruction is filled with the spirit of the Gospel, adapted to the liturgical signs and the cycle of the Church's year, suited to the needs of the catechumens, and as far as possible, enriched by local traditions" (¶16 RCIA).

The retreats that follow offer the catechist or initiation team a variety of options rooted in the Gospels and in the liturgical life of the Church. They include the celebration of the minor rites and opportunities for incorporating local tradition and current signs of the times. From "twilight" retreats lasting for a couple of hours to weekend retreats, these gatherings are truly "suited to a spiritual journey of adults" (¶5 RCIA).

Certain assumptions underlie the design of this resource book and are fundamental to the understanding and implementation of the retreat outlines.

1. The Rite of Christian Initiation is designed for adults who have already been touched by and have responded to the work of God in their lives.
It is God's work that we tend; we support, encourage, reflect, and respond to the signs of emerging life. Clock and calendar have no part in this tender task; it takes as long as it takes. We provide the environment in which that life can be brought forth, but for each individual it is "by God's help [that] they will be strengthened spiritually during their preparation and at the proper time they will receive the sacraments fruitfully" (¶1 RCIA).

This assumption challenges us to be humble and to relinquish any illusion of our own control over the process.

2. The Rite of Christian Initiation is designed on the principle that the work of the catechumenate is "the responsibility of all the baptized" (¶9 RCIA).
It is not the work of the pastoral team, the director of initiation or the team, or a certain group of ministers within the parish community. "The entire community must help the candidates and the catechumens throughout the process of initiation" (¶9 RCIA). The variety of ministries and offices called for by the Rite bears this out, and the primary minister of initiation clearly is the assembly. Within the structures provided by the parish for the catechumenate, it is a matter of justice to call forth and support all of the baptized as ministers of initiation. It is a matter of justice both to the sacramental life of the Church and to the individuals who seek baptism and full communion.

This assumption calls us to cooperation, collaboration, and creativity.

3. The Rite of Christian Initiation is designed for unbaptized adults.
The dignity of the baptized is to be celebrated, and the distinction between baptized candidates and catechumens seeking baptism is to be clear, obvious, and honored. "[Candidates'] status differs from that of catechumens, since by baptism they have already become members of the Church and children of God. Hence, their conversion is based on the baptism they have already received, the effects of which they must develop" (¶400 RCIA).

This assumption challenges us to be theologically sensitive and to be flexible.

4. The Rite of Christian Initiation is designed as a liturgical process that bears a "markedly paschal character" (¶8 RCIA).

It includes "not simply the celebration of the sacraments of baptism, confirmation and eucharist, but also all the rites belonging to the catechumenate" (¶2 RCIA). It can be a challenge for ministers of initiation, particularly those with a background in catechetics or education, to understand and implement the rite as a liturgical process. It means knowing and living the rhythm of the Church's liturgical year in worship and in action. The pattern of Jesus' dying and rising becomes the pattern of the formational process and ultimately the pattern of life and meaning for each of the baptized. Every liturgical celebration derives from and leads to the great Easter Vigil: Sunday to Sunday, source and summit, word and action, sacrament and sending forth, communion and mission, dying and rising—these are the elements of liturgical catechesis when the Church initiates new members.

Because the catechumenate calls for liturgical catechesis, regular celebrations of the Word and the minor rites are essential to the process. The minister of initiation must accept the role of presider and become competent in liturgical language and ritual.

This assumption calls us to ongoing formation to develop competence and to nurture a liturgical spirituality.

LIFE LESSONS

Allow me to share a few vignettes from my own life. Each experience taught me something important about how we are to be as ministers of initiation. What attitudes of heart and aptitudes for pastoral implementation bring life and integrity to the Rite of Christian Initiation of Adults? These simple daily moments became springboards of learning for a lifetime of ministry.

Focus. Clarity. Purpose.

Once upon a time, on a winter day in Alaska, I boarded a small jet to travel from Juneau to Ketchikan. As I settled into my seat, a lovely young family of four boarded: mother, father, toddler, and babe in arms. The toddler was clinging to his father and crying out as loudly as humanly possible for such a tiny person, "I want my blankie! I want my blankie!" The embarrassed parents kept reassuring him that he could indeed have his blankie once he was seated on the plane. Settling the family took longer than our little toddler could handle, so the screaming continued until the pilot of the plane in his spruced-up uniform walked back to the boy, looked him in the eye, and asked, "Well, where are you going today?" The child stopped, sat up straight and tall, focused directly on the pilot, and in a clear, confident voice announced, "I'm going home." That was it: "I'm going home!" and everything was OK.

How important it is for us not to lose focus about what we are doing and where we are going. It is too easy to get caught up in the proverbial "blankies" of security, the externals that comfort or reassure us along the way. The ministry of Christian initiation is hard, complex, and challenging, and only by keeping our focus will we do justice to its implementation. Where are we going? We are going home—to the reign of God. We are journeying always and again from font to table to do what Jesus did. We are going home, creating as we go a little more justice, a little more peace, a little more of the reign of God. Baptism calls us home. Eucharist calls us home. It's often a journey through pain and suffering and death, but through this journey of faith together, we're going home.

Care. Competence. Consistency.

Once upon a time, when my niece Maggie was not quite four years old, she and I sat together playing quiet games while her older sister practiced for a school play. We played hand games, whispering games, and then we played "Who loves you?" games. "Who loves you, Maggie?" The list was long … Mommy, Daddy, Emily, Grandma, Grandpa, Lily (the dog, of course), and so on. Once again I asked, "Who loves you, Maggie?" "You do!" she exclaimed. Departing from the ritual of the game, I followed up with, "How do you know?" "Because you always take very good care of me," was her wise and wonderful reply.

As ministers of initiation we are called to take very good care of many things. We have been entrusted with and are responsible for the very good care of the sacramental life of the Church. Our love for the Church's liturgy is shown in our careful tending of the implementation of the Rite. It is so important for us to know the ritual text well and to be consistent in our pastoral and liturgical practice. The integrity of the process of initiation in all its dimensions—liturgical, catechetical, pastoral, canonical, personal, and communal—demands and deserves our "very good care."

Care includes competence. No one person can offer all the competencies of all the dimensions of this sacramental process. The Rite assumes a variety of ministers, a variety of gifts, a variety of competencies. It assumes pastoral adaptation according to culture, custom, and need. However, adaptations should be made with great care, and the consistency of implementation throughout the Church is to be guided by the ritual text itself.

People. Assembly. Participation.

Once upon a time, I was working with a priest friend preparing for the Easter Vigil in a very small rural community in southeast Alaska. We worked diligently, cleaning the little mission church, discussing the readings, preparing a fire in the snow, creating a baptismal font from a large salad bowl and rocks and leafless branches that we had collected from the surrounding forest. We decorated the assembly space with more branches, set up the folding chairs surrounding the altar, and placed the beautiful new paschal candle, which had been donated by friends in the "Lower Forty-eight," in the center of the assembly's seating. And then we waited. And waited. And waited. No one came. There was no assembly. There was no Easter Vigil.

Liturgy, and therefore initiation, is truly the work of the people. Without the participation of the assembly in the full sacramental life of the Church, there is no full sacramental life of the Church. When we ministers commit our time, effort, and energy to planning and preparation (as well we should!), we must also ask ourselves about our willingness to recognize and facilitate the role of the assembly throughout the catechumenal process. Initiation is neither the work nor the privilege of the pastoral team, the initiation team, or a particular group of ministers within the parish community. No assembly participation? No Christian initiation.

Experience. Revelation. Sacrament.

Once upon a time, the well loved bishop of Juneau, Michael Kenny, died suddenly while on vacation in Jordan. He had embraced the people of southeast Alaska with unbounded tenderness, compassion, and a great gift of humor. He was a bishop in love with his people and they with their bishop. Michael's funeral liturgy was indeed noble in its simplicity, eloquent in its earthiness and symbolic language, richly human and dignified, fully participative in its ritual song and action, and inclusive in its gathering of people from various cultures, faith traditions, and lifestyles. Shortly after the funeral, I received a note from Cardinal Roger Mahony, who, on the same day he had buried his own mother, traveled to Juneau to preside at Michael's funeral. "The flow of the liturgy was so reassuring and hopeful for all of us," he wrote. "I was really able to experience the promises of Jesus Christ in the way that the liturgy unfolded so beautifully."

Isn't that what initiation is all about? Baptism, confirmation, and Eucharist are not goals to be reached or things to be accomplished. Sacraments are a way of being in which our human experience reveals something about who God is and who we are meant to be. Human experience becomes sacramental experience when we have the eyes and ears and heart to recognize it as such. The sacramental dynamic of revelation and response is personal, interactive, and human as well as divine, mysterious, and transformative. We need to believe in the Incarnation if we are to love and trust the liturgical process of initiation. We believe in a God who reveals who God is through human experience and whose revelation is celebrated in the rites. We find meaning and life in the rites that reflect and celebrate real, ordinary, human moments and carry us beyond the obvious and present reality. Something of truth and life and the mystery of God that we call "paschal" is revealed. Song and silence, procession and proclamation, word and gesture, environment and icon, sign and symbol—all become part of God's revelation when we gather to celebrate in faith.

ATTITUDES AND APTITUDES

Initiation is a liturgical—and therefore ritual—process. The best ritual makers are those who are deeply in touch with their own humanness and the rhythms of their own lives, and who have themselves responded to their own felt need to mark significant events, transitions, and life passages. What were the rituals when you were growing up in your family of origin? What are your personal rituals today? To what family or community rituals are you committed? Have you chosen them intentionally, or are you simply going through the motions? Either way, they have an effect on you. What effect do you desire?

It is easy to approach ministry from a dichotomous viewpoint, separating the human from the divine, the secular from the sacred, the mundane from the holy, the worldly from the spiritual. How sad! God has, in a most amazing and creative gesture, shown us something entirely different. "And the Word became flesh and lived among us" (John 1:14).

According to the Gospel, Jesus, the Son of God, chose to take on this skin of ours and then to make water and lilies, tax collectors and prostitutes, lepers and widows, women and children, light and bread and wine, all become the revelation of God. This is where we find communion with God! The Incarnation teaches us that this is the pattern of God's relationship with us.

The minister of initiation must, then, be at home in her or his own skin. We must affirm the "skin" of each person with whom we journey. We must celebrate and honor the sacred "in my skin" stories of the catechumens and candidates. Remember that initiation is a process, and the ceremony is a moment in that process of revelation and response, encounter and conversion. All the conversations, discussions, silences and songs, activities and gestures and prayers are actually part of the full celebration of initiation. A perfectly rehearsed and executed rite will be just that—a ceremony. It may even make a good memory and lovely pictures. But it cannot, in and of itself, either form or express the reality of the living Church praying what it believes and believing what it prays. That belief is the stuff of life, lived and reflected upon.

The sacramental life is our opportunity to do now what we are called to do for all eternity: to be caught up in the dying and rising of Christ and to share in the heavenly table, where there is plenty of bread and no stranger. Therefore, while we "wait in joyful hope," we need to bring to our ministry of initiation our best daily efforts at carrying the cross, dying and rising, washing feet, weeping and working for unity and justice, forgiving and welcoming, including and accompanying the stranger and the friend. Only then will the experience of the Church's sacramental moments create a foretaste of the reign of justice and peace in the life to come. Only then are we more than mere spectators of fairy tales of the future.

Skills for implementing the Rite of Christian Initiation are important. Underlying those skills, however, are the attitudes and aptitudes that transform skills into pastoral ministry, which itself becomes part of the revelation response dynamic of the sacraments of initiation. What can we do to attend to ourselves and our own development as ministers of initiation?

- Attune your own heart to be sensitive to the movements of God within you and the other.

- Be open enough to respond in your most human, creative, and compassionate manner.

- Cultivate a sensual awareness—to light, sound, color, taste, smell—and challenge yourself to discover the revelations that are contained in human experience.

- Be attentive and attend to the moments when you are immersed in water, bathing babies or comforting a dying friend; when you are setting the table and shopping for bread or sharing a glass of wine; when you are making up or feeling sorry; when the leaves are falling and when the flowers are blooming.

- Know the cross as yours today and believe in the Resurrection now.

- Develop the eyes with which to see the world as God does, where the human and the divine are one, and where the Incarnation, the Passion, and the Resurrection are all over the place. When you see the world and other people that way, you will be able to share that vision with others that they, too, may experience rituals in life and life in rituals.

- Stretch your imagination so that the words on the pages of the ritual text get up like dry bones and take on life and dance around in your heart and mind and take on new possibilities.

- Play and celebrate often and with a grateful heart.

THE ROLE OF THE INITIATION MINISTER

Each of the retreats in the following chapters flows from a celebration of the Word of God. The outline and supportive notes for the retreat will give you ideas for facilitating the experience. Essential to the experience, however, is your understanding of your role as a minister of initiation. It is you, as leader, who will bring the ideas to life in your time and place, your cultural milieu and particular circumstances. To what are you called as you incorporate these retreats into your catechumenal process?

You are called to be the Church's storyteller, inviting catechumens and candidates to immerse themselves and discover themselves in the ongoing story of God's loving covenant with the people of Earth and, in a particular way, with the Church. Newcomers to our faith community have been drawn by experiences and stories—their own and others'—of how we live out our faith in God, in Christ Jesus, and with each other who call ourselves Church, for the life of the world. Through these stories they "enter the way of faith and conversion as the Holy Spirit opens their hearts" (¶1 RCIA).

Primacy of place is given to the great stories of God in the Liturgy of the Word. It is the gathered people of God who form the womb in which the Word of God is to be made flesh. In the dialogue of proclamation and response, the words of creation, promise, liberation, reconciliation, salvation, resurrection, and mission become living and active. They have the power to touch hearts and change lives. Together, ministers of initiation, catechumens, and candidates in the liturgical assembly hear the reign of justice and peace proclaimed, and are challenged to make "thy kingdom come, thy will be done" by their own actions and manner of life.

You are called, too, to provide celebrations of the Word that invite catechumens and candidates more deeply into a "profound sense of the mystery of salvation in which they desire to participate" (¶75.1 RCIA). You are called to be presider, proclaimer, and preacher of the Word, providing a solid foundation for the formation of catechumens and candidates.

The Church surrounds the proclamation of the Good News with an abundance of celebratory sights, sounds, symbols, and gestures. God touches us now through tangible, earthy signs and symbols, inviting us to be at home deep in the heart of God, who literally took on our flesh to be at home with us. Gathering, walking in procession, touching, blessing, water, oil, light, bread, wine, giving, forgiving, receiving, eating, drinking, proclaiming, listening: all this, the stuff of life, invites us not only to hear the stories of God but to enflesh them and to make them live again in our own time and place. The Word challenges us to pray as we believe, to believe as we pray, and to live as we pray and believe.

You are called, then, to facilitate the breaking open of the Word and reflection on the experience of the gathered assembly. Reflection on the Word and liturgical action calls us to move from Word to action in doing the work of the gospel, the work of justice and compassion. The liturgy is lived and life is brought to the liturgy.

The Word of God, proclaimed, explained, and lived, is meant to direct the heart toward God, foster participation in the liturgy, inspire apostolic activity, and nurture a life completely in accord with the spirit of Christ (¶78 RCIA). What can undermine these God-centered, community-supported, and mission-oriented goals is a lack of understanding about how, when, why, and for whom the Scriptures were written. It is your call—your responsibility—to help catechumens and candidates hear the Word in context, including the context of its historical roots as well as the context of the liturgical year, the present day, the signs of the times, and cultural and political nuances.

"Catechists should see that their instruction is filled with the spirit of the Gospel" (¶16 RCIA). Literalism, historicizing, and fundamentalism deaden that spirit. Individual faith sharing, personalizing, and situational interpretation may be very important starting points for reflection, but these retreats and all catechumenal processes must move beyond them to a more informed and theologically grounded understanding of the Word of God, living and active in our lives.

Your ministry is for the catechumens and candidates; it is also for the growth of the entire community of faith. Ultimately, however, it is for the mission of Jesus. Your work is to help make the connections between hearing the story of God and being changed by that story (conversion), and between conversion and doing the story (mission). Your work is to help make the connections among what happened in the story/tradition, what is happening in today's story (personal, family, civic, world, cosmic), and the fulfillment of the story in the life to come. The story of God is the story of the reign and the power and the glory of justice over oppression, good over evil, peace over violence, inclusion over discrimination, reconciliation over retribution, life over death—all when it seems impossible. Your work is to keep before the Church the question, "How do we make this possible?" Your work is then to help us make the connections between that question and our baptismal commission. Together, we create the answer as we discover our stories in the story of God and the life of the Church.

Finally and fundamentally, in your own person you are called to be an incarnation of the story of God in Jesus and in the Church. You are called to be a witness to the fidelity of God to all people, and to the dream of God for all people. It is your privilege to hear the catechumens' stories and to discover with them the connections between their own reflected experience and Scripture, tradition, Catholic worship, doctrine, practice, social teaching, and apostolic activity. You are called to wonder with each of the catechumens and candidates about gospel living and eucharistic justice and what we, the Church, are called to in this time and in this place. You are responsible, then, for your own theological and spiritual growth as you journey with those in the initiation process. Know and learn from formational and educational resources, develop skills that will enhance your pastoral practice, and, above all, make a personal commitment to this ministry.

If catechumens and candidates "are expected to have undergone a conversion in mind and in action and to have developed a sufficient acquaintance with Christian teaching as well as a spirit of faith and charity" (¶120 RCIA), your ministry within these retreat experiences and beyond needs to respond to the whole person. Be patient, discerning, and creative. Something precious and unique is unfolding. Tend tenderly. These retreats are offered to enable you and those with whom you minister to enter the process more fully.

Retreat Formats

Leader notes will guide you through the retreat with suggestions for adapting it to your own situation. In some cases, suggestions for particular music selections are given. You are encouraged to use these retreats as guides for your own creativity and to adapt them according to your own style and expression. This is a book of resources, not recipes, and they are offered to support and inspire you. They will come to life only with your own creativity, enthusiasm, and commitment to tend tenderly to the ministry of initiation.

The Context
The Context offers an introduction to each retreat. It highlights its place in the liturgical year and provides its particular focus. Context describes its appropriate use within the process of initiation.

Word of God
The selected readings upon which each retreat is based will be highlighted in Word of God. This section also includes some theological and/or scriptural background about the selected readings.

Sacred Space
For each retreat there are suggestions for creating a sacred space, an appropriate environment for prayerful reflection. Sacred Space offers ideas for decor, images, and focal points for prayers.

Living Rite
Several retreats include the minor rites. Each retreat incorporates some ritual gesture. Living Rite offers suggestions and support for the catechist or retreat leader serving as presider at the rites.

Chapter Two
The Period of Evangelization and Precatechumenate (Inquiry)

The garden is planted.
Beneath the soil, life is stirring.
Unnoticed, the rose takes root
and thrusts its shoots upward,
reaching for the sun.
Small green leaves begin to form.
The rose is alive, growing,
yearning for its fullness.
How long until the full bloom?
It will take as long as it takes.

THE PERIOD OF EVANGELIZATION AND PRECATECHUMENATE (INQUIRY)

Officially, the Rite of Christian Initiation begins with the Rite of Acceptance into the Order of Catechumens. It truly begins, however, when the inquirer, moved by the action of the Holy Spirit, seeks to know God in Christ Jesus and in the Church. The initial period of inquiry is essential to the journey of faith as a time of evangelization when "the living God is proclaimed and Jesus Christ whom he has sent for the salvation of all. Thus those who are not yet Christians, their hearts opened by the Holy Spirit, may believe and be freely converted to the Lord and commit themselves sincerely to him. For he who is the way, the truth, and the life fulfills all their spiritual expectations, indeed infinitely surpasses them" (¶36 RCIA).

Guidance for the period of the precatechumenate is found in ¶42 of the ritual text. It is a time for the "beginnings of the spiritual life and the fundamentals of Christian teaching [to take] root in the candidates" (¶42 RCIA). During this time, noticeable changes take place in each person: evidence of growth in faith, of initial conversion, and of a new relationship with God in Christ Jesus. "Consequently, there must also be evidence of the first stirrings of repentance, a start to the practice of calling upon God in prayer, a sense of the Church, and some experience of the company and spirit of Christians" (¶42 RCIA). All this takes time—as long as it takes.

- The retreats for this period provide opportunities for the initiating community as well as the inquirers themselves to reflect on their faith journeys in light of the articulated goals for the precatechumenate.

- The first retreat is a twilight retreat for Advent. It focuses on the revelation of God in Christ Jesus through the eyes of John the Baptist, Mary, and Elizabeth as models and mentors in faith.

- The second retreat is a two-hour twilight retreat that invites inquirers into the spirit of Lent. It is inspired by the story of the widow of Zerephath.

- The third retreat is an all-day (six-hour) retreat designed for inquirers, initiation team members, potential sponsors, and godparents. It is based on John 21 and is intended to support the discernment process prior to the Rite of Acceptance into the Order of Catechumens.

Advent Twilight Retreat for Inquirers

The Context

The twilight retreat for inquirers is a two-hour gathering prior to or at the beginning of Advent. It is intended for both baptized and unbaptized inquirers who have not been catechized. It is also appropriate for those who have been in inquiry for some time as well as for new inquirers. Members of the parish community may also be invited to participate in the retreat, offering presence and support while encouraging the inquirers to share their stories and insights. For some inquirers, this may be the first introduction to the mystery of the Incarnation. For most, it will probably be the first introduction to the concept of the liturgical year. It is not necessary to "teach" these topics. The retreat provides an opportunity for inquirers to become aware of the movement of the Advent season and to become acquainted with three Advent models and mentors in faith: John the Baptist, Mary, and Elizabeth.

Word of God

An adapted "message" from each of the Advent figures will provide the scriptural foundation for reflection. The leader is the "storyteller" in this retreat—it is not necessary to enthrone the scripture or read directly from the book of the Gospels.
John the Baptist: "Prepare the way of the Lord" (Matthew 3:3).
Mary: "My soul magnifies the Lord, and my spirit rejoices in God my Savior ... The Mighty One has done great things for me, and holy is his name" (Luke 1:46–47, 49).
Elizabeth: "Blessed are you among women, and blessed is the fruit of your womb" (Luke 1:42).

Sacred Space

Prepare the gathering space using the liturgical colors of Advent. You may wish to add pine branches or holly berries. Avoid using Christmas images or decorations. Open the Scripture to the beginning of the Gospel according to Luke and place it on the prayer table or altar. A simple sculpture of Mary may be added to the focal point for prayer.

Living Rite

Provide a transition from the sharing in faith to the closing prayer such as an invitation to stand together in a circle, to move to a chapel or prayer room, or to dim the lights and spend a few moments in quiet reflection. The prayer lends itself to chant and/or sung response. You may wish to invite the participants to use gesture with the spoken or sung response, perhaps lifting hands high and then bringing them close to the heart as you pray "Be with us, O God." The leaders should pray the litany slowly and reflectively, offering the concluding prayer with hands in the orans position.

GATHERING AND SETTING THE CONTEXT
(20 minutes)

Begin with introductions if appropriate. Invite each person to share a brief story about one "new beginning" that has been important to her or him. Give some examples, such as beginning a new job, getting married, becoming a parent, starting college, starting a diet, or beginning to inquire about Catholicism. Share a personal example from your own life.

(10 minutes)

Talk briefly about how new beginnings and anniversaries of important events tend to make us a little more reflective, a little more aware of ourselves and other people. New beginnings are opportunities for making things better for others and for us. They are full of possibility and promise.

Leader *(in these or similar words)*:

You are welcome this evening to our first twilight retreat of this new year. We are beginning the season of Advent, the new year according to the Church's own calendar. We begin once again to celebrate all that we believe as Christians. We believe that Jesus is the Son of God, our Savior. We believe that the scriptures tell us the story of God's relationship with humanity, and that God's personal, unconditional, compassionate love was made visible in Jesus, our Savior.

During Advent, we remember God's promise to send a Savior who would bring liberation and peace to the world. The Savior has come; we celebrate his birth at Christmas. Advent is a time of preparing to celebrate the birth of Jesus.

But still we wait. We are still in need of liberation and peace. We need God's saving action in our lives and in our broken world this very day. Advent is a time of preparing ourselves to receive the love of God into our own hearts day by day.

And still we wait, because our whole lives are filled with a yearning that only God can satisfy. We wait in joyful hope for the fulfillment of all our desires and longings, and that one day everything will be right, good, and alive forever. Advent is a time to look forward to the life that is to come when we reach our heavenly home with God.

Remembering the birth of Jesus, opening our hearts to receive God's love this night, and looking forward to the promises of the future, let us gather in song.

GATHERING SONG

Select an appropriate gathering song or Advent hymn. Keep it simple! The text of "O Come, O Come, Emmanuel" is quite complex and may not be the best choice for inquirers who are probably unfamiliar with its imagery. There are some instrumental versions of the familiar melody (such as the one by Mannheim Steamroller) that could be used for reflective background music during the gathering time.

PRESENTATION
(10 minutes)

Leader:

Each year when members of the Church gather for worship on the Sundays of Advent, we hear scripture stories about three persons who are models or mentors for us as we grow in our own faith. John the Baptist was the cousin of Jesus. His work was to announce to the people that Jesus, the Savior of the world, was coming. John is depicted in the scripture as a very colorful character who lived in the desert, ate locusts and wild honey, and lived a rather transient life. He spent a lot of time preaching by the Jordan River, telling the people to repent of their evil ways because the Lord was near. His message was clear and echoes through the centuries right up to our own time: prepare the way of the Lord! Prepare the way of the Lord! His message is as urgent today in our own lives and in our world as it was when he preached it so many years ago. There is still so much that needs saving. We call to mind victims of war; hungry mothers and children; the gifts of the earth and the environment; the fragile peace that exists in people's hearts, in families, and in some countries. We hear the message "Prepare the way of the Lord!" and know that our own hearts need to be touched and opened so that God can enter. We know that God wants to find the way to our hearts and lives, and we are asked to prepare the way.

(Pause for a moment of reflection)

Mary was the young woman who was chosen to be the mother of Jesus, the Savior. Although she suffered greatly because those who loved her most did not understand what was happening, she had great faith in God. No matter what happened, she saw herself as God's loved one. She recognized her dependence on God. Even though she had the greatest privilege ever given to any human being, the privilege of being the mother of the Savior, she never put the focus on herself. The scripture tells us the lovely story of how Mary totally surrendered herself to God even though she had a lot of questions, and then she turned her attention to helping others. In fact, she set out over the hill country where she lived and walked the long distance to visit her cousin who was also pregnant. When she and Elizabeth greeted one another, Mary's heart was filled with gratitude to God that spilled over into a beautiful song of praise: My soul magnifies the Lord, and my spirit rejoices in God my Savior . . . The Mighty One has done great things for me, and holy is his name" (Luke 1:46–47, 49).

(Pause for a moment of reflection)

Elizabeth was Mary's cousin. She was quite a bit older than Mary was and she was also pregnant, despite her advanced age. Her child would be named John. Through the scriptures we have come to know him as John the Baptist. When Mary visited Elizabeth's home, the two women embraced. Elizabeth was overjoyed to see Mary. The child within her womb seemed to jump for joy when Mary arrived. Elizabeth felt that and knew that this visit was like no other; she was humbled to be in the presence of this lovely, graceful young cousin. The scripture story tells us that she recognized that something miraculous had happened to Mary and suddenly she understood that Mary was pregnant with the promised Savior. Acknowledging the amazing child that Mary carried within her, Elizabeth greeted Mary with profound honor and respect "Blessed are you among women, and blessed is the fruit of your womb" (Luke 1:42).

(Pause for a moment of reflection)

John, Mary, and Elizabeth each have something to tell us about our own Advent journey. They each model for us how we might live as we wait—for Christmas, for understanding ourselves better, for a greater understanding of Christianity, for membership in the Catholic Church, or for whatever we await and long.

REFLECTION AND JOURNAL WRITING
(30 minutes)

Invite inquirers and others present to take advantage of the quiet time to consider the questions provided and to write their responses. During the reflection you may wish to provide soft instrumental music. Invite inquirers to use the reflection time to learn something about themselves and their journeys. They may use the questions provided to direct their reflections and responses.

During this reflection time, the leader and other support people remain attentive to each person and engage in personal conversation with inquirers who may need additional encouragement or direction.

Questions for Reflection and Journal Writing

Prepare the way of the Lord (Matthew 3:3).
The work of John the Baptist was to prepare the way of the Lord by announcing his coming.

- Who are some of the people who have helped prepare God's way in your life?

- What events or experiences have shown you that God is near to you? To our world?

- What events or experiences make it difficult for you to believe that God is near?

- Who or what could support you on your journey? What would help "prepare the way of the Lord" for you?

My soul magnifies the Lord, and my spirit rejoices in God my Savior . . . The Mighty One has done great things for me, and holy is his name" (Luke 1:46–47, 49).
Mary recognized her dependence on God and rejoiced in God's goodness to her.

- When have you been aware of your dependence on God?

- What causes you to rejoice in God?

- What are some of the great things God has done for you?

"Blessed are you among women, and blessed is the fruit of your womb" (Luke 1:42).
Elizabeth joyfully greeted Mary with profound honor and respect.

- Who are some people of faith in your own life whom you honor and respect? Why?

- What experiences have you had of being joyfully greeted by our church community?

- What gift of life does our world (family, community, Church, civic, and social environment) need from you?

My soul magnifies the Lord

Sharing in Faith
(30 minutes)

Invite participants to select one of the three reflections to share with the group. Encourage active listening, not discussion. After each person has shared, invite the group into a moment of silence in order to honor and show reverence for that person's story.

If there is time, repeat the sharing for a second and third time.

Summarize by commenting on common experiences, insights, and themes.

INVITATION TO PRAYER
(10 minutes)

Invite the inquirers to respond to the prayer with the refrain "Be with us, O God."

Leader:

We open our hearts and pray:	R/. Be with us, O God.
When we forget that you are near:	R/. Be with us, O God.
When we need help and support:	R/. Be with us, O God.
Because we depend on you:	R/. Be with us, O God.
Because we rejoice in you:	R/. Be with us, O God.
Because you do great things for us:	R/. Be with us, O God.
As we honor and respect one another:	R/. Be with us, O God.
As we recognize the goodness in each other:	R/. Be with us, O God.
As we greet one another in peace:	R/. Be with us, O God.

Leader:

John the Baptist, Mary, and Elizabeth,
we pray that you will walk with us on our Advent journey of faith.
Be our models and mentors.
Teach us to see how good and near God is to each of us.
Teach us to celebrate God-with-us.
Holy is God's name, now and forever!
Amen.

May God bless us and keep us and give us a peaceful rest this night!
Amen.

Conclude with an appropriate song.

You may choose to make available the scripture citations for the current liturgical year's Sunday gospels of Advent. The inquirers may want to read them on their own and bring their questions and insights to the next gathering.

Lenten Twilight Retreat for Inquirers

The Context
This two-hour retreat invites the inquirers into the penitential season of Lent in anticipation of the promise of the Resurrection. The scripture and rituals of the Lenten season focus on the renewal of all the baptized and on the elect in anticipation of their sacramental initiation. Inquirers and new catechumens have different needs as they are introduced to the Lenten experience for the first time. This retreat provides an opportunity for inquirers to enter into the spirit of Lent as they reflect on what is lacking in their own lives and on what it means to turn away from sin and embrace a spirit of repentance. As they begin to understand the spirit of repentance, they are called to focus not on themselves and their sinfulness but on God's boundless love, and to respond to God's initiative and grace. Because we are not enough on our own, God offers us mercy and forgiveness. Jesus came that we might be made whole again. Dying, he destroyed our death, and rising, he restored our life. Thus, the true spirit of repentance embraces and celebrates the gift of salvation.

Word of God
In the seventeenth chapter of the first book of Kings, the story of the widow of Zarephath illustrates how naming one's "not enough" opens the heart to the gratuitous gift of God. This woman had not enough to feed herself or her child, and together they faced certain death. Even in her poverty, however, she was asked to give what little she had and life was restored and renewed.

Before the reading is proclaimed, it is important to introduce the widowed woman from Zarephath as someone real, someone with whom the participants can identify, someone whose life experience resonates with their own as they struggle to acknowledge and accept that none of us is "enough" and God is All.

Sacred Space
On a table in the center of the room, or on purple fabric draped on the floor in the middle of a circle of chairs, display some dry sticks, a bowl of flour, a cup of water, and a container of oil. You may wish to add a lantern or candles. Use some of the sticks to create a resting place for the scripture. Around the sacred space, place the Lenten cloths, candles, or other Lenten symbol you have chosen to give to each participant at the end of the evening retreat (see "Living Rite" below).

LIVING RITE

This retreat depends on the use of images and the proclamation of scripture. In preparation, the leader should become very familiar with the symbols in the sacred space and with the scripture passage. The proclamation is meant to be in the style of "storytelling" in a relaxed, easy, and reverential manner.

At the concluding ritual, the participants will be invited to share an action plan for Lent. In advance, prepare a simple purple cloth, small purple candle, or other Lenten symbol to give to the inquirers as they name their action plan.

You may wish to incorporate an appropriate Lenten song into this retreat.

GATHERING
(10 minutes)

Begin by welcoming the inquirers and introducing the new season of the Church's liturgical year.

Include these concepts:

Lent is a sacred season.

Lent is a new moment in the Church's liturgical year.

Lent is more somber, quiet, and reflective than the other seasons; however, it is a season of anticipation.

We enter into Lenten practices with joyful hope as we prepare for the great central feast of the Church; Easter.

Even the seasons of nature remind us that spring follows winter, that life comes from death, that light comes out of the darkness.

During Lent, the Church helps us to acknowledge the darkness in our own lives and to be ready to open ourselves to the Light of Christ as we respond in love to the great gift of salvation.

The liturgical color that signifies the season and spirit of Lent, a spirit of repentance and anticipation, is purple.

SYMBOLS AND REFLECTION
(20 minutes)

Invite the participants to reflect on each of the symbols and to select one that most represents how they come to this gathering. Ask them to write a brief reflection in their journal before they are asked to share it with the group.

Give the following examples:

Dry Sticks: You may feel a little, dry, brittle, not sure about continuing this journey of faith or entering into this season of Lent. You may feel broken or guilty, or you may feel all the potential of bursting into a fire of love and service, expressing the power of your faith journey.

Oil: You may feel the need for physical, mental, or spiritual strength in a particular area because of what is going on in your life at this time. You may feel a strong sense of having been chosen, called to be here for a special reason or to give a particular gift to this community, or you may feel unworthy of all that has been given to you.

Flour: You may feel useless by yourself because you're just not enough. You may feel excited by the possibilities of blending with new ideas, people, insights, and ways of being as you continue your journey of faith—or you may feel a bit unsure, bland, and dry, without a sense of where God is leading you.

Wherever you are, whatever your experience is, let these symbols speak to you. Select one of them to tell your story as you are in this place at this time.

SCRIPTURE PREPARATION AND REFLECTION #1
(10 minutes)
1 Kings 17:10–16

Thank the participants for their sharing and give the following introduction to the proclamation of the scripture in these or similar words:

We invite into our circle one more person this evening. She is the mother of one son. Her husband has died, leaving her with very little. She looks at what she has and knows that it is simply not enough. She wants to live, but she has not enough. She wants to feed her son, but she has not enough. It is she who will be our model and mentor this evening as we reflect upon and ponder two differing realities: the gifts we have to share and the sense of "not enough" that often overwhelms us in the face of our sinfulness and weakness. Like each of us at times, she felt that she did not have enough to give in the face of what was being asked of her. She was not sure that she was up to the challenges and demands that faced her. Let's meet her and learn from her.

With reverence and solemnity, take up the scripture, which has been resting in the sacred space in the center of the group. Tell the story slowly and reflectively with expression.

REFLECTION
(10 minutes)

Invite the participants to reflect in silence and then to write in their journals something that touched them, surprised them, or challenged them as they listened to the reading.

BREAK
(10 minutes)

SCRIPTURE PROCLAMATION #2 AND REFLECTION
(20 minutes)
1 Kings 17:10–16

Invite the participants to reflect for a moment and then to share with the group what they are learning for their own lives from the widowed woman of Zarephath.

FAITH IN ACTION
(20 minutes)

Guide the participants to consider what gifts they have to share, just as the widow from Zarephath shared her little bit with the visitor Elijah.

Remind them that God does not expect us to have "enough," but we are asked to name what is lacking in us and to share what we have with others. Encourage them to consider gifts of the heart and spirit as well as material gifts.

Assist the inquirers in identifying programs or groups within the community with which they can share their gifts (e.g. a homeless shelter, a women's shelter, children's advocacy programs, housing projects, etc.).

At the end of this discussion, invite them to make an action plan for the Lenten period and write it in their journals. What will each person do as a sign of repentance and gratitude during this season? Let the inquirers know that they will be asked to share some aspect of their action plan during the closing prayer.

CONCLUDING PRAYER
(20 minutes)

Address each inquirer by name or address the group in these or similar words:

____, you will be able to provide more than enough for others if you give freely and generously of what you have, even when it is not enough. What will you do as a sign of repentance and gratitude during this Lenten season?

INDIVIDUALS RESPOND.

Following each response, invite the person to take from the sacred space the Lenten symbol you have prepared in advance as a reminder to live Lent in the spirit of repentance and gratitude.

PRAYER
Leader:
Let us pray.
Accept our gifts, O God,
not enough though they be,
and transform them into plenty to share
with our sisters and brothers in need.
Accept our gratitude for your love and grace,
and help us to respond to you with free hearts.
Give us and our world, we pray,
plenty of knowledge and wisdom,
plenty of justice and compassion,
plenty of bread and peace.
You are the one true God, forever and ever.
Amen.

DISMISSAL
Leader:
Let us go now in peace,
knowing that while we are not enough on our own,
God gives us all that we need.
Let us give generously from what we have.
Let us enter into this Lenten season with gratitude.
Let us go now in peace.

Invite the participants to offer each other a sign of peace.

Do you want to be totally united to the Crucified?

If you are serious, you will be present, by the power of His Cross, at every front, at every place of sorrow, bringing to those who suffer, healing and salvation.

Blessed Edith Stein

Discernment Retreat Prior to the Rite of Acceptance into the Order of Catechumens

The Context

This retreat is designed for inquirers who have been in the precatechumenate for an extended period of time and are ready to discern their call to the Rite of Acceptance into the Order of Catechumens. This retreat is also appropriate for baptized inquirers who have not been catechized and are seeking to be welcomed into full communion with the Catholic Church.

It is a full-day retreat that can be extended to a weekend retreat or divided into several sessions. It includes the inquirers, their potential sponsors, the initiation team, the pastoral staff, and members of the worshiping community. Based on the post-Resurrection story of Jesus greeting Peter and asking him, "Do you love me?", the retreat guides the participants through reflections on Paragraph 42 of the Rite of Christian Initiation of Adults, which describes readiness for the Rite of Acceptance:

> The beginnings of the spiritual life and the fundamentals of Christian teaching have taken root in the candidates. Thus there must be evidence of the first faith that was conceived during the period of evangelization and precatechumenate and of an initial conversion and intention to change their lives and to enter into a relationship with God in Christ. Consequently there must also be evidence of the first stirrings of repentance, a start to the practice of calling upon God in prayer, a sense of the Church and some experience of the company and spirit of Christians (¶42 RCIA).

By the time inquirers are ready for this retreat, they are familiar with some of the ritual and symbolic language of the Church: enthronement of scripture, proclamation and response, the sign of the cross, ritual dialogue (including responses to readings and greetings), and the greeting of peace.

Prior to the beginning of the retreat, meet with the potential sponsors and other support persons separately in order to encourage them to participate fully in the process. Emphasize that their role during the dialogue sessions is to listen, to reflect what they hear back to the inquirer, to clarify, to encourage, and to assist the inquirer in greater awareness of the movement of God in her or his life. It is not their role to teach, to judge, to preach, or to make decisions about the inquirer's readiness for the Rite of Acceptance.

WORD OF GOD
JOHN 21

The post-Resurrection narrative in John 21 forms the basis of this discernment retreat. Sometimes called the "epilogue" or later addition to the Gospel of John, this chapter places before the Church the challenges of discipleship after the earthly life of Jesus of Nazareth. The images of the fishing expedition, the breakfast meal of bread and fish, Peter's profession of love, and Jesus' commissioning of Peter provide an appropriate scriptural framework for reflection and discernment on readiness for the Rite of Acceptance into the Order of Catechumens.

SACRED SPACE

Because of the length of this retreat, it is advisable to consider a retreat house site or similar environment apart from the usual gathering space. The primary focal point for prayer includes the enthroned scripture and a simple wooden cross, perhaps surrounded with blue fabric and seashells.

The retreat day is held as sacred time. Suggested time frames are given for each element of the retreat. The day should also include a morning break of at least twenty minutes, an afternoon break of at least twenty minutes (these could be silent breaks), and a meal break of at least forty-five minutes.

LIVING RITE

The proclamation of the Word is surrounded with acclamation, procession, and ritual dialogue. It is important for the leader to take the role of presider seriously and to create a smooth transition from reflection and dialogue sessions to the liturgical moment of celebrating the Word of God. This may be accomplished through song, silence, gesture, a location change, or a clear verbal invitation to enter into the sacred moment of proclamation. It might also be helpful to designate one person to be the retreat facilitator and another to serve as the presider for the rituals.

Each part of the suggested ritual is modeled on and prepares inquirers for the liturgy of the Church, which they will experience as catechumens and candidates. It is important, therefore, to celebrate these rituals well, by tending to detail with "noble simplicity" and by avoiding minimalism.

GATHERING
(10 minutes)

Welcome the inquirers, sponsors, initiation team, pastoral staff, and members of the community who will be participating in the retreat day. Recognize in a particular way those who are here to discern their next steps in their journey of faith, both those who are on their way to entering into the catechumenate and those who have been baptized and are seeking full communion with the Catholic Church. Remind all present that this day of discernment is a time for the participants to reflect on their relationship with God in Christ and in the Church, and to reorient themselves to the movement of God's Spirit within each one and among all gathered.

Invite them to participate fully, allowing God's Word to live in them, challenge them, guide them, and support them as they reflect on their journey of faith thus far.

GATHERING SONG
Begin with a simple, appropriate song.

OPENING PRAYER
Leader *(with hands in the orans position):*
Loving God, you have called each of us by name.
We believe that you are with and within us,
loving us into life and calling us to embrace the way of the gospel.
Guide us through the gift of this day;
show us your will and your way.
Open our hearts and minds to hear and understand your Word.
May your Word become the story of our lives.
We ask this through Christ our Lord, who lives and reigns with
you in the unity of the Holy Spirit, one God, forever and ever.
Amen.

PROCESSION AND PROCLAMATION OF THE WORD
Sing a simple Alleluia as the scriptures are held high in a procession through the assembly. The use of incense may be appropriate during the procession.

PROCLAMATION OF JOHN 21:1–14

PRESENTATION
(In these or similar words)

Believing in Jesus and his resurrection is always a matter of faith. This was as true for the early disciples as it is for us. The Gospel we have just proclaimed tells us that Jesus takes the initiative and reveals himself in the ordinary activities of our daily lives. For the early disciples, it was during a fishing trip. For each of us, it is a different and individual story of time and place. For all of us, there was a moment when we recognized that God was indeed involved with us, present with us, calling to us.

We decided to get into the boat and found ourselves with some companions. And together we began to explore our experience—our successes and our failures, the times when our net of life was full of hope and blessing and peace, and the times when it was totally empty, bringing us disappointment and discouragement. Reflecting on our experience together, asking questions, learning the scriptures, and being in each other's company led us to recognize the power and presence of Jesus in our midst.

Each response to the revelation of Jesus is individual and unique. Peter recognized Jesus and jumped into the water with his clothes on. Some of us are impulsive, some of us much more reflective, some simply slower at responding or resistant to making a decision.

But Jesus' desire to reveal himself to us and to be faithful to us does not fail; he waits for us on the seashore or wherever he find us. He invites us into an intimate relationship with him, to get to know him, even to share meals with him. What a wonderful experience that morning breakfast on the beach must have been! How excited the disciples must have been when they recognized him as they ate the bread and the fish.

The image of the disciples of Jesus gathered together believing—knowing—that Jesus was there with them is an image of us gathered here together believing—knowing—that he is with us and wants to share that same spirit and company with us. He invites us to gather around his Word in his presence. The Church gathered is a place of fullness. Our work today is not to catch one hundred fifty-three fish, but to discover more fully the meaning of Jesus' presence in our lives.

REFLECTION
(30 minutes)

Invite the participants to reflect on the following questions in their journal:

- When and how have I recognized the revelation of Jesus in my life?

- What are the events, persons, or experiences that have contributed to my journey of faith? How?
  (RCIA ¶42: Initial conversion and revelation of Jesus Christ)

- How has the company of Christians in this church community touched me? Changed me? Challenged me?
  (RCIA ¶42: The spirit and company of Christians)

- When do I experience my "net of life" being full of hope, blessing, and peace? When do I experience it being totally empty?
  (RCIA ¶42: Sense of sin and repentance)

DIALOGUE
(30 minutes)

Invite the inquirers to partner with another participant (potential sponsor, team member, or member of the worshiping community) to share their responses.

GROUP CONVERSATION
(15 minutes)

Invite the participants to share with the group any questions or insights that emerged from their dialogue session. During the conversation, answer questions as appropriate while keeping the focus on the key elements of initial conversion and relationship with God in Christ.

BREAK

Procession and Proclamation of the Word
Sing a simple Alleluia as the scriptures are held high in a procession through the assembly.

Proclamation of John 21:15–19

Presentation
(In these or similar words)

The encounter between Jesus and Peter in this Gospel is written to show both the reason for and the cost of discipleship. The reason is love. The cost is the cross.

Peter had denied that he even knew Jesus before his death on the cross! Notice that Peter's denial, certainly a cowardly and sinful act, did not keep him from continuing his relationship with Jesus. Notice that Jesus still chooses to be present to Peter and to meet Peter where he was, doing his daily work at the seashore. And notice that his relationship with Jesus led Peter to repent and trust in the Lord's love and forgiveness for him. Now, in this story about Jesus after the Resurrection, Peter is invited to profess his love for the risen Lord. Jesus asks him over and over, three times, "Do you love me?" Three times Peter says, "Yes." And three times, Jesus gives Peter a commission. He tells Peter that he must do something to show his love; he must be about the work of taking care of others. Peter's love for God will be shown in action, not words. It will become a lifestyle for Peter.

Those who love God are called to share in the mission of Jesus as Peter was.

What is important to the risen Jesus is that the people of this world be taken care of by his disciples: "Feed my lambs . . . Tend my sheep" (John 21:15, 16). What is important is that believers show their love in actions that make a difference in this world. Sharing in the mission of Jesus is the work of the Church: to do what Jesus did—bringing healing, justice, forgiveness, joy, and peace into the world—by who we are and how we live.

That work, that kind of life, will sometimes take us where we don't want to go. We will be faced with our own crosses and trials. Jesus makes it clear to Peter that following him means following him to the cross as well as to the Resurrection. The only thing that makes it possible for us to accept that cross is love. We are invited, like Peter, to give our response in freedom and love. Do you love me? Will you follow me? Will you share in my mission? Will you accept my cross?

Reflection
(30 minutes)

Once again invite the participants to reflect on the following questions in their retreat journal and to write their responses:

- I am invited, like Peter, to respond in freedom and love: Do you love me?
  (¶37 RCIA: Drawn into the mystery of God's love; ¶42 RCIA: First faith, entering into a relationship with God in Christ)

- Will you follow me? What does following Jesus mean for me now?
  (¶42 RCIA: Repentance, fundamentals of Christian teaching)

- Will you share in my mission? In what ways can I share in the mission of Jesus?
  (¶42 RCIA: Spirit and company of Christians, sense of the Church)

- Will you accept my cross? What does accepting the cross mean to me?
  (¶42 RCIA: Spirit of Christians, initial conversion)

Dialogue
(30 minutes)
   Invite each inquirer to share her or his responses with the same dialogue partner as before.

Group Sharing
(30 minutes)
   Invite each pair to join with other pairs to form groups of no more than six people. Invite them to talk together about the questions and their responses.
   After sharing, invite the participants to voice prayers for each other in their groups.
   (¶42 RCIA: The practice of calling upon God in prayer)

Break

Proclamation of John 21:20–25

Presentation
(In these or similar words)
   The story of Jesus and the disciples, particularly Peter, is our story, too. Each time we hear it we are reminded of the reason for our own choice to follow Jesus. We are reminded, too, of the cost of being a follower of the risen Lord. We, like him, will be asked to carry our own crosses in life. We will be asked to show our love in action. The final section of the Gospel tells us that, like Peter, we will also have to take responsibility for our own discipleship. We will be asked not to worry about what others are doing or saying, but to be true to our own call from God. Jesus is very clear about what he asks us to do: "You follow me." Don't be concerned about other things and people and what might happen to them. "You follow me."
   In the final verses of this Gospel, the writer expresses what we know to be true: there is just so much to know about Jesus, and there is so much involved in learning to know him and his church. The whole world could not contain the books that could be written concerning this knowledge of Christ and the church. The way to know the risen Lord and his church is through relationship. Being with him in prayer, individually and when we gather as a community of faith; being in the company of other believers; listening to and pondering his Word proclaimed; seeking reconciliation; living according to the values of compassion and justice that he preached and lived—these are ways we encounter the risen Jesus in our lives today, just as concretely as Peter and the other disciples encountered him after his resurrection.
   The gospel is written so that we may believe. There are also many other things that Jesus does, and for the rest of our lives, let us continue to discover them, accept them, and celebrate them.

REFLECTION
(30 minutes)

Invite participants to consider prayerfully the following questions, which are found in their journals. Call their attention to the fact that they are being invited to write a simple prayer response of their own. They will be asked to bring their prayer to the closing ritual.

- We are asked to be true to our own call from God.
  What am I being called to at this time in my relationship with God? With Christ Jesus? With the Church?

- Jesus says, "You follow me."
  Am I being called to follow him as a member of this faith community?
  What is my response?

PRAYER RESPONSE

Invite the inquirers to write a simple prayer response that expresses what is in their hearts at this time.

Invite other participants to write a simple prayer for the community of faith, particularly for those who are interested in learning more about the Catholic Church.

CONCLUDING RITUAL
(30 minutes)

GATHERING SONG
(perhaps repeat the gathering song from the first ritual)

OPENING PRAYER
Leader:
Lord Jesus, we have walked with you today
just as Peter and the disciples walked with you.
We have heard you call us to follow you.
We thank you for the freedom you give us
to respond each in our own way.
As we continue to grow in faith and love,
help us to recognize and accept your cross and resurrection in our lives.
Give us courage to accept the gospel as the story of our lives.
We make this prayer in your name, Jesus, our Lord forever and ever.
Amen.

PROCESSION AND PROCLAMATION OF THE WORD

Sing a simple Alleluia as the scriptures are held high in a procession through the assembly. If possible, form a procession of the entire assembly and move to a special place for the final proclamation of the Gospel.

PROCLAMATION OF JOHN 21:1–25

SILENT REFLECTION

RESPONSE

Invite the inquirers to share their prayer responses with the group.
If there is time, you may also invite the other participants to share their prayers.
After each person shares, sing or say together an acclamation such as "Blessed be God" or "Blessed be God who calls you by name. You are holy and chosen in God's sight!"

BLESSING

Invite all the participants to form a circle.
Leader:
Bow your heads and pray for God's blessing. *(pause)*
Leader *(with hands extended in blessing)*:
May God bless us and keep us.
May God's face smile on us.
May God look upon us with kindness
and give us deep peace.
Amen.

Leader:
Let us offer each other a sign of peace.
An appropriate concluding song of praise may be sung.

29

Chapter Three
Catechumenate

The bud appears.
Life pulses through the rose.
The unfolding begins.
Slowly, gradually,
almost imperceptibly,
the bud opens to the sun above.
Enter the rose!
Believe in its beauty.
Discover its mystery.

CATECHUMENATE

"The catechumenate is an extended period during which the candidates are given suitable pastoral formation and guidance, aimed at training them in the Christian life" (¶75 RCIA). During this time, catechumens are immersed in the Word of God, in the life of the community of faith, in the liturgical and ritual life of the Church, and in apostolic activity that bears witness to their faith.

According to the National Statutes for implementation in the United States, the catechumenate lasts for at least one year. However, because conversion is a gradual process that is unique to each person and circumstance, it will take as long as it takes. The purpose of the catechumenate is to initiate catechumens into the life of faith, worship, and service that characterizes the community of disciples of Jesus Christ. For this reason, instruction alone is not sufficient; initiation is a process that "directs the heart toward God, fosters participation in the liturgy, inspires apostolic activity, and nurtures a life completely in accord with the spirit of Christ" (¶78 RCIA).

The heart of the matter for the catechumenate is the celebration of the Word of God. During the course of a liturgical year, through the liturgy of the Word, the Church presents the core mysteries of faith including the Incarnation, the Paschal Mystery, the life and teachings of Jesus Christ, and the mission of the Church guided by the Holy Spirit. The transformation that takes place for catechumens as they become more and more familiar with the Christian way of life is blessed, affirmed, and supported by celebrations of minor rites: exorcisms, blessings, anointings, and special celebrations of the Word of God appropriate to their formation.

The retreats in this section are designed to draw the catechumens more deeply into the mysteries of faith and to support them as they discern their call to discipleship as members of the Catholic faith community. The first two retreats in this section are appropriate for candidates as well as catechumens. The third retreat is a day of discernment for catechumens prior to the Rite of election.

The first retreat is a Twilight Retreat that incorporates the minor rites belonging to the period of the catechumenate. The script serves as a "template" for a variety of retreats that could take place throughout the catechumenate and offers guidance for the leader to create original evening retreats appropriate for individual groups and circumstances.

The second retreat is a Marian retreat designed as a daylong experience or as a series of "prayer hours" over a period of several weeks. For many catechumens, this will be the first introduction to a theological understanding of the role of Mary in the Church and in their lives.

The third retreat is designed as a day of discernment prior to the Rite of election. It draws the catechumens into an exploration of their faith journey and uses the criteria for election (¶120 RCIA) as a guide for the content of the retreat.

Twilight Retreat: The Rites Belonging to the Period of the Catechumenate

THE CONTEXT

Formation during the period of the catechumenate includes celebrations of the Word of God, the minor exorcisms, the blessings of catechumens, and the anointings of catechumens. The design of this twilight retreat provides the catechist or retreat leader with a flexible structure for creating a twilight retreat appropriate for catechumens at any time during the liturgical year and according to local circumstances. The retreat evening comprises an extended celebration of the Word of God with time for reflection as well as the celebration of the minor rites. The structure of this retreat, which includes the key elements of liturgical catechesis and the minor rites, should be used frequently throughout the period of the catechumenate.

The catechist or retreat leader should become very familiar with the section on "Rites Belonging to the Period of the Catechumenate" from the *Rite of Christian Initiation of Adults*:

    Celebrations of the Word of God (¶81–89 RCIA)
    Minor Exorcisms (¶90–93 RCIA)
    Blessings of the Catechumens (¶95–96 RCIA)
    Anointing of the Catechumens (¶98–101 RCIA)

If you choose to include candidates in the retreat experience, keep the distinctions between the catechumens (unbaptized persons) and candidates (baptized persons) clear. The minor rites are for the catechumens; they are part of their sacramental baptismal journey. You may wish to include a special prayer and/or blessing for the candidates; a sample is included in the retreat script. Another option is to use the "Order of Blessing for a Catechetical or Prayer Meeting" from the *Book of Blessings* published by the United States Conference of Catholic Bishops.

WORD OF GOD

The Liturgy of the Word is the centerpiece of the retreat. Readings should be selected with reference to any or all of the following criteria:

    Seasons and feasts of the liturgical year
    Cultural feasts
    Local and global current realities
    Catechetical and formational needs of the catechumens

Suggestions include planning a Liturgy of the Word focused on the Beatitudes, the Ten Commandments, the parable of the good Samaritan, the teaching of the Our Father, the Annunciation, the conversion of Nicodemus, or the story of Pentecost from the Acts of the Apostles. These suggestions highlight passages that have strong catechetical elements appropriate to the formation of catechumens. There are, of course, many other possibilities.

Sacred Space

The primary images for the catechumenate are the cross and the Gospels. Regardless of feast or season, these images ought to be part of the focal point for prayer. They may be enhanced with fabric appropriate to the season: green for Ordinary Time, blue-violet for Advent, purple for Lent, white for Easter, red for Pentecost. You may wish to add simple earth images such as plants, water, candles, rocks, shells, etc., especially if they have some relationship to the word that will be proclaimed. If you choose a Marian reading, it would be appropriate to add an image of Mary that has particular meaning to the people in your community.

Living Rite

It is important that a person competent in liturgical prayer preside at the Liturgy of the Word for this retreat. Each rite included in the retreat should be celebrated fully, lavishly, and with dignity. The presider should prepare well in advance and work with the lectors and musicians to plan an integrated and effective celebration of the Word. RCIA ¶85–89 outlines a structure and guidelines for a celebration of the Word of God.

As prescribed by the Rite of Christian Initiation of Adults, the minister for the celebration of the Word of God, the minor exorcisms, and blessings of the catechumens may be a qualified catechist, and the minister for the anointing of the catechumens is an ordained deacon or priest. The structure provided here and the options for prayers and blessings are found in the *Rite of Christian Initiation of Adults*. Creativity and adaptation in ways that may enhance the spirit and intent of the rites are encouraged as catechists and presiders become familiar with the minor rites.

Gathering

Select a gathering song appropriate to the liturgical season or the focus of the reading for this particular celebration.

Greeting

(In these or similar words)

We gather for this evening of prayer and reflection, pausing for a while to reflect on our journey of faith. We will hear God's word calling out to each of us, teaching us, guiding us, challenging us, encouraging us to live according to the gospel that we accepted as our way of life at our celebration of the Rite of Acceptance. Whether we look forward to the day of baptism into Christ Jesus, or celebrate the baptism we have already received, we believe that God speaks to us this evening in our gathering.

Let us make ourselves ready to hear God speak through the word proclaimed, in the movement of the Spirit in our own hearts and minds, and through the prayer of the Church. Let us pray that God's word will inspire us to act with compassion and justice as we strive to live as faithful disciples.

OPENING PRAYER
Leader:
Let us pray. *(pause, and then pray with hands in the orans position)*

Select or create a prayer appropriate to the liturgical season or feast, selected scripture, and local circumstances.

READINGS AND RESPONSORIAL PSALMS

"One or more readings from scripture, chosen for their relevance to the formation of the catechumens, are proclaimed by a baptized member of the community. A sung responsorial psalm should ordinarily follow each reading" (¶87 RCIA).

If a Gospel is proclaimed, sing a Gospel acclamation and process with the Gospel book before proclaiming the chosen passage.

HOMILY

Offer a brief reflection, prepared in advance, that draws the catechumens and candidates more deeply into the scripture that has been proclaimed, and helps them make connections between the Word proclaimed and the Word lived in their own lives.

REFLECTION AND JOURNAL WRITING

Invite the catechumens and candidates to spend a period of time in private reflection on the scriptures. Encourage them to write in their journals in response to the following questions:

- In the Word proclaimed, what touched you, surprised you, challenged you, or raised questions in you?

- What is the scripture that you heard proclaimed saying to you, personally, at this time in your life?

- To what do you believe this scripture is calling you? To what do you believe this scripture is calling us, the Church?

- How can our faith community support you in your faith journey?

SHARING

The facilitator for the group sharing could be someone other than the presider. Invite the catechumens and candidates to gather for sharing. In large groups, divide the participants into smaller circles, and then invite each circle to share something about its responses to the last two questions.

INTERCESSIONS

The presider stands and by gesture invites the catechumens and candidates to stand for prayer, saying, "Let us pray."

After a pause for silent prayer, the presider says a short prayer asking God to hear the prayers of the people gathered together in faith.

You may choose to have prepared intercessions. However, this is a good opportunity to invite the participants to articulate their prayers for the needs of the Church and the world. For each intercession, use a sung or spoken response that is familiar to your faith community.

MINOR EXORCISM

Invite the catechumens to come forward and kneel. Invite someone to hold the Rite of Christian Initiation ritual book for you so that your hands are free.

Address the catechumens in these or similar words:

Leader:
Pray now for the strength and courage to continue your journey of faith, even in times of struggle and doubt.

Pause briefly.

Let us pray.

Pray with hands outstretched over the catechumens, selecting a prayer from the Rite of Christian Initiation of Adults, *in the section on "Minor Exorcisms."*

ANOINTING OF THE CATECHUMENS

Invite the catechumens to stand and gather around the oil of catechumens as the priest or deacon prays the prayer indicated in the Rite of Christian Initiation of Adults, *in the section on "Anointing of the Catechumens."*

The priest or deacon anoints each catechumen individually. The anointing may include the hands or other parts of the body according to cultural custom, norm, and sensitivity.

BLESSING OF THE CATECHUMENS

Following the minor exorcism (and the anointing if it is included in the retreat experience) the presider prays the prayer of blessing with hands outstretched over the catechumens. The prayer should be selected from the options provided in the Rite of Christian Initiation of Adults, *in the section on "Blessings of the Catechumens."*

Following the prayer of blessing, the presider may lay hands on each catechumen individually, praying in silence.

BLESSING OF THE CANDIDATES

If you choose to include a blessing of the candidates, use one of the options below or create a similar blessing appropriate to your situation.

OPTION 1

The presider may call forward the baptized candidates and invite them to kneel as a blessing is prayed over them in these or similar words:

Leader:
O God, gracious and merciful One,
in the waters of baptism you claimed these, your children, as your own.
You called them by name and shared with them the gift of new life.
Strengthen them in faith.
Free them from all that would keep them from you.
Send your blessing upon them that the grace given to them in baptism
will be brought to completion by your love and power.
This we ask in the name of Jesus, our Savior and Brother,
who is Lord forever and ever.
Amen.

Option 2
Use the "Order of Blessing for a Catechetical or Prayer Meeting" from the Book of Blessings *published by the United States Conference of Catholic Bishops.*

Following the prayer of blessing, the presider may lay hands on each catechumen individually, praying in silence.

Dismissal
After the catechumens have celebrated the minor rites, the presider dismisses them and the candidates in these or similar words:

Leader:
We have heard the Word of God.
We are called to live the Word of God.
We have been blessed and strengthened by our gathering here
and in our celebration of the rites of the Church.
Go now in peace.
Proclaim the Word by your words, your actions,
and your manner of life,
In the name of God our Creator, of Jesus, our Redeemer,
and of the Holy Spirit, Source of all life,
one God forever and ever.
Amen.

Concluding Song
Select a concluding song appropriate to the liturgical season or the focus of the reading for this particular celebration.

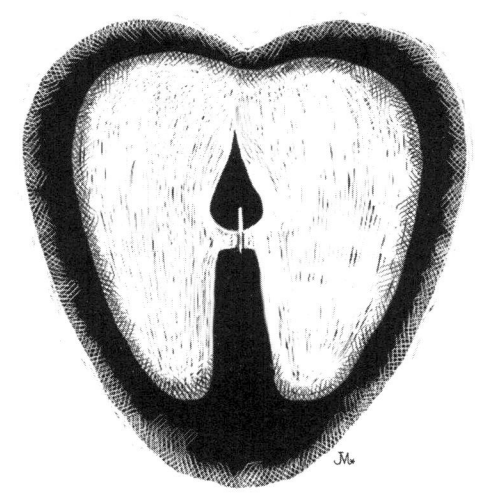

Marian Retreat for the Catechumenate

The Context
As catechumens seek to learn more about the liturgy, practices, and devotions of the Catholic Church, devotion to Mary can become anything from a fascinating attraction to a stumbling block. This retreat is designed to give catechumens and candidates the opportunity to reflect on Mary's role in the Church and in their lives. (The content of this retreat is influenced by *Mother and Disciple* by Charles E. Miller, CM, and writings by Paul Ford, PhD, and Sandra Schneiders, IHM.)

This retreat may be held at any time during the catechumenate. It is appropriate for catechumens, candidates, sponsors, and other parishioners. It may be useful to offer this retreat near a Marian feast, during the month of May or, depending on cultural feasts celebrated in your local situation, at another time when the catechumens and candidates are likely to be introduced to Marian devotions.

The retreat as designed takes a minimum of four hours. It may be extended to an all-day retreat or divided into several "prayer hours" over the course of several weeks.

Word of God
Three passages will be highlighted during this retreat: the Annunciation (Luke 1:26–45), the wedding feast at Cana (John 2:1–12), and the Crucifixion (John 19:25). Each of these passages highlights an aspect of discipleship modeled by Mary: opening ourselves to the action of God in our lives (our baptismal call); sharing Christ with others (our Eucharistic mission); and offering everything through, with, and in Christ, to God in fidelity and hope (our worship).

Outward expressions of devotion to Mary vary according to different ages, cultures, stages of faith development, and popular piety. What remains constant in the Church, however, is the fact that devotion to Mary is for the purpose of union with Christ, and is meant to draw us into full, conscious, active participation in the liturgy, which is source and summit of the Church's activity.

Sacred Space
The environment may be set up to include a statue, icon, sculpture, or other image of Mary. Select an image that is culturally appropriate to your community or a modern image that in some way emphasizes her relationship with Christ Jesus. There are many contemporary images that depict Mary as a woman from the Middle East would appear today or that show her interacting with her child and Joseph, her husband.

Use traditional blue fabric and flowers to enhance the space. Create a prominent place where the scripture can be enthroned. Keep the space simple. Do not add rosaries or other devotional items, but plan to address questions about them in a follow-up catechetical session.

The final section in the retreat journal offers the option for drawing, symbolizing, or writing a personal response. If possible, provide materials such as paint, crayons, markers, tissue paper, glue, etc. Encourage the participants to be creative in their responses, and to attempt to create a prayer response in an art form in place of a written expression.

LIVING RITE

The ritual for this retreat should be simple, scripture-based, and focused on the relationship between Mary and the Church. It should honor Mary as the model for our own discipleship. Chapter 36 of the *Book of Blessings* provides an "Order for the Blessing of an Image of the Blessed Virgin Mary," which may be used or adapted as a closing ritual. The retreat script offers several other options for a closing ritual. The selection should be made according to the feast or season of the year, sensitivity to local culture, and the practices and needs of the local community.

Three times during the retreat, a passage from scripture will be proclaimed. Each time, the leader should reverently approach the sacred scripture, bow, raise the book high, open it, and proclaim the word with clarity and strength.

GATHERING
(30 minutes)

Welcome the participants to this time of retreat. If the group does not gather on a regular basis, take time for introductions. Direct the participants to focus on the sacred space that holds the image of Mary, and ask this question:

What thoughts, feelings, or questions emerge as you look at our prayer space today?

Allow time for individual responses. Do not answer questions or enter into discussion. Then invite the participants to enter into this time of retreat.

Include the following points in your remarks:

This retreat is an opportunity to spend time with Mary, to get to know her and her role in our lives and in the life of the Church.

Mary is God's wonderful and creative work of art, a woman of courage and faith, vision and grace. Like us, she was called to be a disciple of Jesus Christ. She was prepared by God to be his mother.

By listening and responding to God's word, Mary shows us what it means to be a blessed disciple.

The tenderness, compassion, love, mercy, and fidelity that we see in Mary are a reflection of God's own tenderness, compassion, love, mercy, and fidelity.

The Church has a long history of devotion to Mary, but not to one particular expression of that devotion.

The aspect of Marian devotion that is essential is that which leads us to do as she did, that is, to make our lives a response to God's will for us and in doing so, to bring the Word of Life into the world for others.

Jesus once said, "Blessed are those who hear the Word of God and obey it" (Luke 11:28). That is exactly what Mary did and what she teaches us to do in good times and in bad.

SECTION ONE

PROCLAMATION OF LUKE 1:26–45
(15 minutes)
Leader:
Let us listen to God's Word and ask Mary to teach us how to be true disciples of Jesus Christ.

Approach the book in the sacred space reverently, bow, raise the book high, open it, and proclaim the Gospel to the gathered assembly with clarity and strength.

REFLECTION

The retreat leader or another person offers a reflection on the scripture in these or similar words:

In this passage, through the greeting of the angel Gabriel, we hear the first prayer ever directed to Mary. This scripture passage is the foundation of the well-loved "Hail, Mary," a prayer that is said during the praying of the rosary and at other times of personal prayer and devotion. We echo Gabriel's greeting to Mary, we call her blessed among all women, and we give honor to the blessed child of her womb. "Hail, Mary, full of grace! The Lord is with you. Blessed are you among women, and blessed is the fruit of your womb, Jesus."

Mary is blessed because of her great trust in God and her willingness to surrender to God's will for her. Without seeing or knowing, she allows the Spirit of God to enter into her life in such a powerful way as to bring forth new life, the Son of God in Jesus, her son. She teaches us that God's Spirit is life-giving and that true discipleship means saying "yes" to the will of God as it is revealed through that same Spirit in our own lives.

In the second part of the prayer we pray, "Holy Mary, Mother of God, pray for us sinners, now and at the hour of our death." Why do we pray to Mary? We pray in faith for the same reasons we pray for one another. We believe in the power of intercessory prayer, prayer on behalf of each other. Prayer is a way of sharing life and grace with each other and our sisters and brothers throughout the world. Just as God chose to come into this world through the woman Mary, God continues to be present to us through each other and through our human experience.

We believe that the power of prayer goes beyond the grave—those who have died still care for us, intercede for us, and are instruments of God's grace for us. We are part of a grand and glorious community, the communion of saints. Mary's place in that communion inspires us to turn to her to pray for us. To our God, to whom we look for our redemption and transformation, we pray, "Lord, have mercy on us!" To Mary we call out, "Pray for us!" as we continue our journey through life, right up to the hour of our death.

Let us reflect on Mary's discipleship, marked by total trust and surrender. Let us remember that, even in the confusion of an out-of-wedlock pregnancy with all its social consequences, including the near loss of her fiancé, she was able to discern God's voice and respond to God's call in faith and with total generosity. "Let it be with me according to your word" (Luke 1:38). Let us ask Mary to teach us how to respond to the voice of God speaking in the circumstances and through the people in our own lives.

JOURNAL REFLECTION
(30 minutes)
Leader:

Mary's discipleship called for total trust and surrender. Even in the midst of confusion, she was able to discern God's voice. We, too, learn to listen to God's voice and sense the movement of God's Spirit in the circumstances, persons, and events of our daily lives.

Invite the participants to reflect on the following questions, which appear in the journal for this retreat. Ask them to write their responses in their journals. Let them know that they will be called to gather in prayer and invited to share their reflections on the "Hail Mary," found on page five of their journals.

REFLECTION QUESTIONS

- Where do I hear the voice of God calling me at this time in my life?
- What motivates me to respond to God's call in faith and with total generosity?

- What makes it difficult for me to respond in faith and trust?

- Who are the people and what are the circumstances that bring God's grace into my life now?

Reflections on the "Hail Mary"

Hail, Mary, full of grace, the Lord is with you.
Blessed are you among women, and blessed is the fruit of your womb, Jesus.
Teach me, Mary, . . .
Holy Mary Mother of God, pray for us sinners, now and at the hour of our death.
Pray for me, Mary, . . .

Prayer Gathering
(20 minutes)

Gather the participants in a prayerful atmosphere. You may wish to use some instrumental music of familiar Marian hymns such as the "Ave Maria" or "Immaculate Mary" as background during the gathering.

Invite the participants to share what they have written in their journals in response to the invocation.

"Teach me, Mary . . ."

The group may repeat the following refrain after each person's sharing:

Hail, Mary, full of grace, the Lord is with you.
Blessed are you among women, and blessed is the fruit of your womb, Jesus.

Invite the participants to share what they have written in their journals in response to the invocation.

"Pray for me, Mary . . ."

The group may repeat the following refrain after each person's sharing:

Holy Mary, Mother of God, pray for us sinners, now and at the hour of our death.

Break
(20 minutes)

Reflection and Introduction to Scripture Proclamation
(10 minutes)

The leader or another person offers an introductory reflection in these or similar words:

Devotion to Mary is most authentic when it leads us to discipleship, to do as she did. In other words, devotion to Mary is one path toward greater communion with God. Our devotion to Mary is most profound when it is reflected through action in imitation of her relationship with Jesus.

The story of the wedding feast at Cana from the Gospel of John recounts Jesus' first miracle, when he publicly manifests that he belongs to God and that his mission is to do God's work. Through Mary we learn that the motivating factor in Jesus' life is doing God's will and acting compassionately for the glory of God. She teaches us that we are to do likewise; we are to do whatever he tells us and whatever he shows us through the action in his own life.

In this passage Mary "lets go" of Jesus and gives him to the gathered community. He does not belong only to her, his mother. He belongs to the people. As is the case with any true disciple, even his mother must share him with others, knowing that he will act in their lives for their greater good and for the glory of God. She is free of heart and totally confident when she tells the people to trust him to do whatever needs to be done to put things right in a confusing and uncomfortable situation. Can we do any less? As followers of Jesus we, too, are called to give Jesus to the community, to invite others to know him and trust him, and to trust that he will put things right even in the most confusing and difficult situations. Like Mary, we must keep the focus on his message and mission, doing all we can to invite others into relationship with Jesus, and then relinquish control, as she did.

Mary is the model of faith, of assertive action flowing from faith, and of simple surrender in her relationship with God through Jesus, her son. Notice, too, that Mary's faith is modeled right in the midst of a great party, a community gathering, a wedding feast of fun, food, and companionship. It is a feast that gives us a foretaste of the heavenly banquet we will all one day share and the eucharistic banquet that awaits us in this community of faith.

SECTION TWO

PROCLAMATION OF JOHN 2:1–12

Approach the book in the sacred space reverently, bow, raise the book high, open it, and proclaim the Gospel to the gathered assembly with clarity and strength.

RESPONSE

After a moment's reflection on the Gospel, sing an appropriate Marian hymn or a version of the Magnificat. In selecting a hymn, be careful to choose something that is based on scripture and is appropriate to the theological and ecclesiological formation of the participants.

GROUP SHARING
(20 minutes)

Lead the participants in a simple sharing of their impressions and understanding of the Gospel.

- What did you hear?
- What challenged you or surprised you, especially about Mary's role in this story?
- How are you called to imitate Mary's discipleship in action?

BREAK
(10 minutes)

PROCLAMATION OF JOHN 19:25
(10 minutes)

Following the break, use a gong, drum, singing bowl, or chimes to gather the participants around the word. Begin with a moment of silence, raise the Scripture high, and proclaim simply and dramatically the single sentence from John's Gospel.

REFLECTION

The leader or another person offers a reflection on the scripture in these or similar words:

Mary's fidelity led her to the cross. Standing there watching her son die, she did not waver. She stayed with him in the face of darkness and death. Although surrounded by other women, including Mary Magdalene and Mary the wife of Clopas, Mary was, in a very real sense, alone. She had every reason to despair, to rage, to blame God, to give up. But she stood there by the cross. The cross that held her dying son was for her the very place that called for her greatest fidelity and her strongest hope. The cross called her beyond the present moment of death into the yet unseen promise of the future. She knew her son and she had followed him and been true to him throughout his life. She was not going to give up on him now. His own fidelity to his God and his message of hope in new life and resurrection gave her strength to be there, to stay there in the shadow of his cross.

The picture of Mary at the foot of the cross is a picture of hope and encouragement for us. It calls us to believe as she did in fidelity to Jesus and to his message. With Mary we are called to embrace the realities of death and darkness with hope. With her, through her son, with her son, and in her son, we are called to offer our own lives to God. We make an offering in Spirit and in truth as Jesus did. This is our ultimate act of worship: to be in communion with Jesus' great act of faith and surrender just as Mary was, and to offer our lives in praise and thanksgiving to God who transforms darkness into light, death into life, and hope into a life of eternal glory.

At the Rite of Acceptance, you accepted the cross. With Mary, supported by this community of faith, you are called to stand by that cross.

JOURNAL REFLECTION AND WRITING
(30 minutes)

Invite the participants to reflect on the following questions, which appear in the journal for this retreat. Ask them to write their responses in their journals.

- When does standing by the cross seem to be just too much?
- What does Mary teach me about hope and fidelity in the face of darkness and death?
- Am I willing to stand by the cross? What does that mean for me at this time in my life?

Invite the participants to draw, symbolize, or write their own creative, personal response to Mary as they have come to know her during this retreat time. This can be done on page nine of the journal for this retreat.

CLOSING RITUAL
(length of time depends on option selected)

There are several options for a closing ritual for this retreat. Select one appropriate for your local circumstances, participants, liturgical season or feast, and parish practices and devotions.

1. "Order for the Blessing of an Image of the Blessed Virgin Mary"
2. Litany of the Blessed Virgin Mary (perhaps inviting the participants to add invocations of their own)
3. The rosary (if that devotion has been introduced at a prior gathering or earlier in the retreat; it may not be appropriate to add the Creed and Our Father if these Presentations have not yet been celebrated with the catechumens)
4. "May Crowning" within the context of a Liturgy of the Word
5. Procession to a shrine or image of Mary at the parish church or grounds, with a proclamation of the Word and intercessory prayer
6. Participation in a parish Marian devotion, liturgy, or special event

OPTIONAL SESSION
(30 minutes)

At this time, if there is a particular Marian devotion that is especially dear to the people of your parish, talk about the image of Mary honored in that devotion. You may wish to select an image according to the cultural practices of your community, a Marian title if she is your parish's patroness, or a popular image such as Our Lady of Guadalupe, the Madonna of the Streets, or Mary, Star of the Sea. Explore the aspects of discipleship expressed through the image or devotion:

- How is Christ Jesus central to this image?

- How does Mary reveal the face of Christ in this image?

- How does this image or devotion draw believers more deeply into the mystery of communion with God and with all the angels and saints?

- What is Mary's role in the Church as seen through the lens of this particular image or devotion?

Discernment Retreat for the Rite of Election

The Context

The rite of election, normally celebrated on the First Sunday of Lent, takes place after a "lengthy period of formation of the catechumens' minds and hearts" (¶118 RCIA). Prior to the rite, there should be a time of discernment for the catechumens' readiness to be called and chosen for the Easter sacraments. The ritual text makes it clear that this discernment process is to be taken seriously and that "election" is a significant step in the catechumens' journey to the font and table. "To exclude any semblance of mere formality from the rite, there should be a deliberation prior to its celebration to decide on the catechumens' suitableness" (¶122 RCIA). This retreat provides the opportunity for the catechumens to reflect on their journey of faith—past, present, and future. The basis for the reflection and discernment questions is ¶120 RCIA, which outlines the criteria for readiness for full sacramental initiation into the Church.

The participants in the retreat are those who have been in the catechumenate for a year or more (#6 National Statutes for the Catechumenate) and who may be ready for the second step toward the sacraments of initiation, that is, the rite of election. Sponsors, pastoral ministers, catechumenate team members, and the pastor should also be present. Their participation in the discernment process in the name of the larger community is significant.

This retreat is a formal time of discernment. It is very important to address any doubts about a person's suitability for election and any canonical impediments to full sacramental initiation prior to this retreat. Sponsors, team members, pastors, and pastoral ministers should be prepared in advance for appropriate participation in the retreat. They need to understand their role in discernment. They are there to listen carefully to each person and to be attentive to the story of conversion that is told. They should have ¶120 RCIA as a "backdrop" for their listening and, if necessary, ask questions for clarification. They should not, however, engage in discussion, correction, disagreement, or judgment of any kind. If concerns about a catechumen's readiness for sacramental initiation emerge, they should be brought privately to the attention of the director of the catechumenate and the pastor.

The duration of the retreat will depend on the number of those in attendance. It is designed as an all-day retreat, but can be adapted easily to a weekend retreat or to a series of evening gatherings.

This retreat is intended for unbaptized persons seeking full initiation through baptism, confirmation, and Eucharist. However, it may be adapted for use with baptized candidates for full initiation. This would require some adjustments in the leader presentations and reflection questions. The exorcism and blessing at the end of the retreat would be omitted and replaced with an appropriate blessing of the candidates. Using the retreat for catechumens and candidates together is not recommended unless there are separate leaders, input, and concluding blessings for each group.

WORD OF GOD

The scripture passage chosen for this retreat is the familiar poem about time from Ecclesiastes 3:1–8: "For everything there is a season." Catechumens have progressed through the seasons of evangelization and initial conversion, followed by the season of deeper conversion through the catechumenate. In discerning their call to live the rest of their lives as fully initiated members of the Church, catechumens are asked to consider their conversion in mind and action. They are asked about their willingness and readiness to make a pledge of fidelity expressing their intention to receive the sacraments of the Church (¶120 RCIA). The Church community joins the catechumens in this discernment process. This retreat supports the discernment process through questions about time. There is a season for everything: is this the season of election for these catechumens?

SACRED SPACE

If possible, arrange to hold the retreat in a space away from the usual place for catechumenate gatherings. A retreat house or other place apart can provide an environment more conducive to the prayer, reflection, and perspective necessary for good discernment.

The cross and the Gospels are the primary symbols of the catechumenate and should be the main focus of the environment for this retreat. A lovely focal point can be created by using the Book of the Gospels and a simple wooden cross surrounded by beautiful fabric and a variety of plants. Keep the environment simple, avoiding the use of other symbols; however, if there is a cultural icon or symbol of particular significance to the group, it can be integrated into the sacred space.

Part of creating sacred space is setting an atmosphere of reverence, respect, and confidentiality. As part of the introduction to the retreat, take the time to talk about the responsibility of each person for confidentiality both during and following the retreat. Journal entries are not to be discussed outside of the guided sharing times designated by the leader. Individual concerns should be represented to the catechumenate director or pastor.

LIVING RITE

This discernment retreat calls the leader and/or presider to be aware of the transitions that occur throughout the reflection, sharing, and common prayer sections of the retreat. The leader will add solemnity to the experience through effective use of body language, tones of voice, presiding style, and facilitation skills. There are several ritual moments that weave the day together. The concluding ritual includes an exorcism and blessing of the catechumens from the ritual text. The centerpiece of the retreat is the Litany of Time. It is woven together by the scripture passage from Ecclesiastes, which may be spoken or sung. There are several musical versions of the text, or a simple plainchant melody can be applied to the text and sung by the gathered assembly. The Litany of Time should be presented creatively, beautifully, and reverently.

GATHERING
(30 minutes)

Welcome the catechumens and sponsors. Include the following points in your welcome:

The rhythm of the Church's liturgical year is bringing us closer to the time of Lent. Lent is a special time of prayer and penance as the Church prepares for the celebration of the Paschal Mystery and the renewal of baptism.

Lent is a time of intense preparation for those seeking the gift of baptism—those who will be called to the Easter sacraments at the Rite of election on the First Sunday of Lent.

Today, each catechumen will be invited into a time of prayer, reflection, and honest dialogue in anticipation of the Lenten season.

As catechumens, they are privileged to be living through a unique and precious time in their lives.

Today presents the opportunity to reflect on their catechumenal experience in terms of their relationship with God in Christ Jesus and in the Church.

Today is a gift of time that they give to themselves, to each other, and to God.

The time spent in retreat today will help them and the Church, guided by the Holy Spirit, to discern God's call at this time in their lives.

Invite the participants to quiet themselves, to be still in God's presence, to open their hearts and minds to the guidance of the Holy Spirit throughout the day.

Use a bell, gong, or singing bowl to introduce each section of this Litany of Time. Invite team members or sponsors to read different sections of the litany. Encourage them to use their voices to "sound like" the words they are reading, expressing the emotion of each phrase.

LITANY OF TIME

**For everything there is a season,
    and a time for every matter
        under heaven:
a time to be born, and a time to die;
a time to plant, and a time to pluck up
    what is planted.**

Play time . . .
Fun time . . .
Work time . . .
Study time . . .
Break time . . .
Lunch time . . .
Stressful time. . .
Happy time . . .
Perfect time . . .
Inappropriate time . . .
Good time . . .
Bad time . . .
Sad time . . .
Sweet time . . .
Slow time . . .
Impatient time . . .

Exciting time . . .
Boring time . . .
Relaxing time . . .
Hard time . . .
Great time . . .
Wonderful time . . .
Abundant time . . .

**For everything there is a season,
    and a time for every matter
        under heaven:
a time to kill, and a time to heal;
a time to break down,
    and a time to build up.**

Fruitful time . . .
Peaceful time . . .
Anxious time . . .
Beautiful time . . .
Distant time . . .
Loving time . . .
Unchanging time . . .
Merry time . . .

Powerful time . . .
Intimate time . . .
Tremendous time . . .
Horrible time . . .
Terrific time . . .
Trying time . . .
Depressing time . . .
Joyful time . . .
Confusing time . . .
Lonely time . . .
Interesting time . . .
Awkward time . . .
Hopeful time . . .
Sacred time . . .
Quiet time . . .

For everything there is a season,
    and a time for every matter
        under heaven:
a time to weep, and a time to laugh;
a time to mourn, and a time to dance.

Noisy time . . .
Exceptional time . . .
Unprecedented time . . .
Tedious time . . .
Crazy time . . .
Silly time . . .
Awful time . . .
Annoying time . . .
Exhilarating time . . .
Refreshing time . . .
Delightful time . . .
Creative time . . .
Foolish time . . .
Emotional time . . .
Suspenseful time . . .
Hurtful time . . .
Awesome time . . .
Fearful time . . .
Fantastic time . . .
Awe-inspiring time . . .
Unsure time . . .
Weird time . . .

For everything there is a season,
    and a time for every matter
        under heaven:
a time to throw away stones,
and a time to gather stones together;
a time to embrace,
    and a time to refrain from embracing.

Endless time . . .
Unmerciful time . . .
Meaningless time . . .
Independent time . . .
Advantageous time . . .
Predictable time . . .
Scary time . . .
Surprising time . . .
Unpredictable time . . .
God's time . . .
Paschal time . . .
Time speeds
Time runs
Time flows
Time flies
Time stops
Time jumps
Time travels
Time tiptoes
Time knows
Time reels
Time carries
Time quickens
Time slows
Time halts

For everything there is a season,
    and a time for every matter
        under heaven:
a time to seek, and a time to lose;
a time to keep, and a time to throw away.

Time wanders
Time ends
Time begins
Time crawls
Time creeps
Time drags
Time lingers
Time freezes
Time pauses
Time moves
Time works
Time continues
Time glides
Time races
Time prolongs

Time heals
Time soars
Time mends
Time changes
Time waits
Time paces
Time leaps
Time nags

For everything there is a season,
    and a time for every matter
        under heaven:
a time to tear, and a time to sew;
a time to keep silence, and a time to speak.

Time lives
Time dies
Time stalls
Time drifts
Time passes
Time accelerates
Time decelerates
Time glides
Time endures
Time empowers
Time ticks
Make time
Give time
Save time
Buy time
Carry time
Watch time
Waste time

Fill time
Honor time
Keep time
Ignore time
Manage time

For everything there is a season,
    and a time for every matter
        under heaven:
a time to love, and a time to hate;
a time for war, and a time for peace.

Celebrate time
Compute time
Plan time
Calculate time
Offer time
Use time
Enjoy time
Remember time
Savor time
Trust time
Suspend time
Desire time
Live time
Love time

For everything there is a season,
    and a time for every matter
        under heaven:

Time is God's blessing.
Time is God's gift.

Reflection
(30 minutes)

Allow for a time of silence following the litany. Then ask:

As you listened to the litany, what did you hear? *(pause)*

As you listened to the litany, what did you feel? *(pause)*

Invite the participants to share their responses with one another in pairs or triads, and then invite them to share with the large group.

Break
(20 minutes)

Presentation
(10 minutes)

Time is a gift. Receiving each day and each moment as a gift opens us to the presence, action, and surprises of God in our lives. One of the most important aspects of our faith is the mystery of the Incarnation. We believe that it is within time that God meets us, touches us, and reveals who God is for us and for the world. The present moment is a sacrament of God's imminent presence.

When we gather as people of faith and members of a worshiping assembly, we find ourselves also immersed in time past and time to come. We remember what God has done for us, and we look forward with joyful hope to the coming of our Savior, Jesus Christ, in the fullness of time. We remember the life, teaching, and mission of Jesus and we look forward to the reign of justice, love, and peace that he promised. We remember Jesus gathered at table with his disciples, and we look forward to gathering at the heavenly table with all the angels and saints to feast forever. That is why, no matter what is happening on any particular day, we can say with the Psalmist every day, "This is the day the Lord has made; let us rejoice in it and be glad" (Psalm 118:24).

You have been given a very special gift of time. As catechumens, you have spent time with this community of faith. For each of you and for all of us, it has been a time of growth, discovery, challenge, and conversion. Now it is time to probe, plumb, explore, and reflect on that experience so that, together, we may discover its meaning for you. There is a time for everything. For some, it may be time to take the next step toward full initiation. It may be time for the Church to call you to inscribe your name in the Book of the Elect and to prepare more intensely to celebrate the Easter sacraments. For some, it may be time to continue the precious journey of the catechumenate. For some, it may be time to respond to God's call in a new and unimagined way. Together, we will seek to discover God's will for each of us at this moment on our faith journey.

Think back to the day you were accepted into the Order of Catechumens. Since that day, how has your time as a member of this faith community deepened your own conversion in mind and in action? What have you learned about Christian living and Christian teaching during this time? How has the spirit of faith and charity made a difference in your life during this time? How have you changed? What do you think, believe, and do because of the time you have spent as a catechumen within this community?

Reflection and Journal Writing
(30 minutes)

Invite the catechumens to enter into silent reflection and to write in their journals in response to the questions below. Let them know that they will be asked to share their responses with their sponsors and the other participants. Explain that a separate handout will be given to those who are not catechumens to assist them in their reflection and discernment. Each group will be praying about the same things, but from a different perspective, so that each person can make an appropriate contribution to the discernment process.

Journal Questions

- How has your time as a member of this faith community deepened your own conversion in mind and in action?

- What have you learned about Christian living and Christian teaching during this time?

- How has the spirit of faith and charity made a difference in your life during this time?

- How have you changed? What do you think, believe, and do because of the time you have spent as a catechumen within this community?

Sharing
(30 minutes)

Invite the catechumens to share their responses. If there is a large group, divide into smaller groups that include catechumens, sponsors, and team members. Do not engage in a discussion. Rather, encourage the catechumens to tell their stories and invite the others to receive each sharing with reverence and respect.

After each person's sharing, invite the group to respond with the traditional Hindu "Namaste" blessing (found on page six of the journal), which honors the presence of God within each person. The blessing song was written by Millie Rieth and is available on a recording and accompanying music book entitled "Namaste." It may be accompanied by a gesture of hands extended in blessing or a more traditional gesture of bowing with hands folded and shoulders bent as a sign of reverence, respect, and humility.

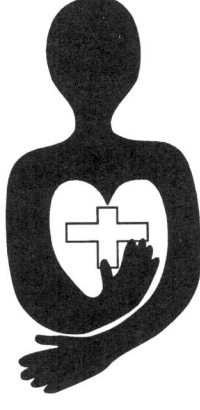

I honor that place in you of light and truth and love.
I honor that place in you where we can be as one in peace and joy.
And when the best in you becomes the best in me as well,
Perhaps the good we wish to see will happen
    when we tell our lives in love.
I bless you forever.

Break
(60 to 90 minute meal break)

Reflection
(30 minutes)

Invite the catechumens into another period of journal reflection in these or similar words:

Our journey of faith is not an isolated, individual experience. We make a public profession of faith. We journey together as members of a community. As one body, we live the mysteries of faith throughout the liturgical cycles and seasons. We express our faith in sign, symbol, and sacrament. We are formed and renewed by the rich heritage of the Church's tradition, ritual, and symbolic language. We learn who we are and we become who we are; we are formed into the Body of Christ, the Church, as we worship and serve together.

JOURNAL QUESTIONS *(found on pages seven through nine of the journal)*

- What has been your experience of the liturgical feasts and seasons?
- What practices and symbols particularly touch you?
- What are the patterns of life or threads of meaning that are emerging for you as you experience the liturgy and practices of the Church?

SHARING
(30 minutes)

Once again, invite the catechumens to share their responses. If there is a large group, break into smaller groups that include catechumens, sponsors, and team members. Do not engage in a discussion. Rather, encourage the catechumens to tell their stories and invite the others to receive each sharing with reverence and respect.

BREAK
(15 minutes)

DECLARATION OF INTENTION
(45 minutes)

Address the catechumens in these or similar words:

We have reflected on your time with us, your time with God—in Christ Jesus and in the Church—as catechumens. You have shared with us how you have listened and responded to God's Word. You have told us your stories of walking in God's presence and bringing the message of the gospel to others through your works of charity and service. You have shared your prayer, your hopes and dreams, your struggles and questions with us. There is a time for everything. What time is it for you? Do you wish to enter fully into the life of the Church through the sacraments of baptism, confirmation, and the Eucharist? Do you believe that you are being called to sacramental initiation at this time? Or, do you believe that you are being called at this time to continue your journey as a catechumen?

To the best of your ability and ours, we now enter into prayerful discernment of God's call to each of you. We seek God's will, not our own. With open hands *(with a gesture of invitation lead the participants to pray with you, hands in the orans position)* **and open hearts, let us ask for guidance, for wisdom and insight, for courage and commitment, for a spirit of openness and peace.**

Pray in silence for a few moments or invite shared prayer.

Then continue in these or similar words:

It is time to respond to the final questions in your journals:

- What time is it for you?
- Do you wish to enter fully into the life of the Church through the sacraments of baptism, confirmation, and the Eucharist?
- Do you believe that you are being called to sacramental initiation at this time?
- Or, do you believe that you are being called to continue your journey as a catechumen?
- What do you ask of God, the Church, and this community at this time?

It is time to express clearly your desires and intentions. You may write a prayer, a letter to the pastor, a letter to the parish community, a personal creed, or use a format that helps you clearly express yourself. These responses will not be shared with the group. Each catechumen will be invited to bring her or his journal to a personal conversation with the pastor, director, spiritual companion, and/or other appropriate persons as the final step in the discernment process. This is sacred time. Receive it as a gift. We will gather for our closing ritual in forty-five minutes.

CONCLUDING RITUAL
(45 minutes)

Use the "Model for a Celebration of the Word of God" (¶85–89 RCIA) to prepare a celebration appropriate for the persons, time, place, and circumstances of this retreat.

Select a Scripture passage that is reflected in the prayer texts that you choose (¶94 RCIA and ¶97 RCIA).

Prepare in advance with the assistance of music ministers, readers, and pastor.

Include the minor exorcism followed by an anointing with the oil of catechumens, as well as an appropriate blessing from the ritual text.

Use the singing bowl, bell, or gong used during the gathering at the beginning of the day to call the group to prayer.

If the catechumens have already celebrated the Presentation of the Lord's Prayer, include the "Lord's Prayer" in the closing ritual.

Conclude the celebration with a sign of peace and a simple dismissal.

Chapter Four
Candidates for Full Initiation

All that life!
All that energy!
All that beauty!
Each petal of the rose
tells a glorious story
of the life
that has been held
within the bud.
The rose begins to bloom,
a magnificent promise
of the fullness to come.
Enter the rose!

CANDIDATES

Candidates are those who have been baptized and are, therefore, already members of the Church. Their formation is based on both acknowledgment and celebration of their status in the Church. Incorporation of baptized but previously uncatechized persons calls for an exploration of the meaning of their baptism through scripture, ritual, prayer, and faith sharing so that the "faith infused in baptism [may] grow in them and take deep root through the pastoral formation they receive" (¶401 RCIA).

The catechesis, rituals, and symbols that are part of the candidates' formation may parallel those of the catechumens; however, there should always be a clear distinction between those preparing for baptism and those who have been baptized. The process of preparation for the completion of Christian initiation should unfold in such a way that the baptism of the candidates is recognized, reflected upon, probed for deeper meaning, and celebrated. The retreats in this section are designed specifically to facilitate the spiritual development of candidates as they prepare to complete their initiation through a profession of faith and/or confirmation and eucharist.

Rituals intended for catechumens only are not to be celebrated with the candidates. They are offered here as preparation for immersion in the baptismal waters. Alternative rituals are included in this section on retreats for candidates. These alternative rituals recall and celebrate the baptism that is already theirs, as well as their membership in the Body of Christ. If you choose to celebrate a combined ritual, be aware of the appropriate wording for catechumens and for candidates.

The first retreat is a three-hour celebration of God's covenant and the call to discipleship. It may be held during Lent or at another time during the year. Figures from scripture are presented as mentors and models in the faith.

The second retreat is a three-hour experience with the Samaritan woman at the well. It may be held during Lent or just prior to the candidates' first celebration of the sacrament of reconciliation, in anticipation of the completion of their sacramental initiation.

Lenten Retreat for Candidates

THE CONTEXT

This retreat is designed for baptized adults who are ready to complete their initiation through the sacraments of confirmation and Eucharist, or who have been preparing to be received into full communion with the Catholic Church. Sponsors may also be invited. Depending on the number of participants, this is a three- to four-hour retreat.

The *Rite of Christian Initiation of Adults* calls for a clear distinction between the catechumens (who are unbaptized) and candidates (baptized persons), and for a "program of training, catechesis suited to their needs, contact with the community of the faithful, and participation in certain liturgical rites" (¶401 RCIA) in order to strengthen them in the baptismal life that is already theirs.

"Once formally welcomed into the life of the community, these adults, besides regularly attending Sunday Eucharist, take part in celebrations of the word of God in the full Christian assembly and in celebrations arranged especially for the benefit of the candidates" (¶413 RCIA). One of these special celebrations is the Penitential Rite recommended for the Second Sunday of Lent. The Penitential Rite itself is contained in ¶464–472 RCIA and should be "adapted in such a way that it benefits all the participants" (¶461 RCIA).

This retreat may be used in preparation for the Penitential Rite or for the celebration of the sacrament of reconciliation. However, it may also be used at any time near the end of the candidates' period of formation as a special time for reflecting on and discerning their call to full sacramental initiation within the Catholic Church.

WORD OF GOD

This retreat celebrates and reaffirms the uniqueness of each person's baptismal call. It honors the individuality of each person's story and invites the candidates to celebrate the journey of faith that has led them to seek the completion of their sacramental initiation. The first reading (Isaiah 62:2b–5) celebrates God's covenant and fidelity. The "new name" given to Israel prefigures the new way of being that each candidate is called to experience and express through full sacramental initiation.

Each person's unique story is also prefigured in some way in the great story of the Gospel. The leader will offer a brief presentation of twelve individuals who were in relationship with Jesus and shared in his life and mission. Candidates will be invited to consider these figures and asked to identify with one of them as a starting point for reflecting on her or his faith story. The journal provides reference citations for the twelve scripture figures, and each candidate will have the opportunity to search the scripture for one of these or another "scripture companion" who will become part of the reflection and sharing segments of the retreat.

Sacred Space

If the retreat is held during Lent, the environment should be simple, even stark, in the spirit of Lent. Use Lenten purple fabric, adding such things as cactus, barren branches, or rocks. Because the entire Church is anticipating the renewal of baptism at the Easter Vigil, baptismal images or icons should not be used. Provide a place to enthrone the scripture or Book of the Gospels as the centerpiece of the environment. A simple wooden cross may also be added.

If the retreat is held at another time during the year, prepare a simple environment appropriate to the season of the liturgical year. You may wish to add a large candle and provide each candidate with a taper to be used during the closing ritual.

Provide a copy of the New Testament for each candidate, placing it in the sacred space until it is needed for private reflection.

Living Rite

The proclamation of the Word is the primary liturgical rite. It calls for simplicity and reverence, because of the reflective nature of this retreat. There is no need for a Gospel procession. Following the proclamation of the reading from Isaiah, provide for an extended period of reflective silence before singing the responsorial psalm. The entire retreat is meant to be a time of prayer, and the leader's demeanor will set the tone and guide the candidates from Word to reflection to sharing to prayer.

If this retreat is being held during Lent, the "living rite" will be celebrated in full in the context of the liturgical assembly during the penitential rite or the sacrament of reconciliation.

If it is held during another season, the closing ritual can be celebrated more fully with the candle-lighting ceremony of renewal.

Gathering
(10 minutes)

Welcome the candidates and their sponsors. Situate the call to retreat in the appropriate context according to the liturgical season and purpose of the retreat. During the Lenten season the retreat is a proximate preparation for the penitential rite or the sacrament of reconciliation. In Ordinary Time or another liturgical season the purpose of the retreat is to reflect on each person's unique story and to make a recommitment to continuing the baptismal journey of faith to full initiation.

Opening Ritual
(20 minutes)

Gathering Song

An appropriate song should be sung.

Opening Prayer

Leader *(with hands in the orans position)*:
Let us pray.
As we gather in your presence, loving God,
we thank you for these, your precious ones,
whom you have called by name
and made your own through baptism.
May we come to a deeper appreciation of this baptismal call.
May we grow to know you, love you,
and serve you with ever greater joy.
May the Holy Spirit, who searches every heart,
continue to draw us closer to you.
Forgive all that keeps us from you and brings hurt to your people.
We place all our hope in you through your Son,
Jesus Christ, our Savior and Brother,
who lives and reigns with you and the Holy Spirit,
one God, forever and ever.
Amen.

Proclamation of Isaiah 62:2b–5

The proclamation should be done slowly, gently, and with passion.

Reflective Silence
(3 minutes)

Responsorial Psalm

Any sung version of Psalm 139 is appropriate.

Group Reflection
(15 minutes)

Guide the candidates in a reflection on the first reading.

- What did you hear?
- What touched you?
- What did you feel as you listened to the reading?

Reflection and Journal Writing
(10 minutes)

Invite the candidates to write in their journals in response to the following questions:

- How have you experienced God's faithful covenant in your life?
- What is the "new name" that you are being called to as you prepare to renew your baptismal commitment and seal that covenant through confirmation and Eucharist?

Sharing
(20 minutes)

Invite the candidates to share their responses. Depending on the number of participants, you may wish to have them share in small groups or with one other person before sharing in a large group.

Break
(15 minutes or meal break)

Presentation
(15 minutes)
(in these or similar words)

We have heard each other's sacred stories. We marvel at the uniqueness of each person's journey. God truly rejoices in you!

It is in Jesus that we discover how much God rejoices and delights in each person. And it is from Jesus that we learn how faithful God is to each of us, regardless of the meanderings and side trips we might take along our individual journeys of faith. Baptized into Christ, we have each taken a unique path in our life. None of us has the same story. Our personalities, circumstances, and challenges have been and will continue to be unique. But we all have the same desire, that is, to deepen our relationship with Christ and to participate fully in his mission through full participation in the life and sacraments of the Church. No, none of us has the same story, but we share a desire to renew our baptism, when we were called by name and drawn into the mystery of Christ's love, life, death, and resurrection. What will it cost each of us to say "yes" to that call?

The models and mentors we find in the Gospels and Acts of the Apostles are as unique as we are. Unique personality traits, circumstances, and challenges determined each one's relationship with Jesus. Diverse paths brought each one to a common center: intimate relationship with Jesus and participation in his mission. Let's consider a few of them in particular and, in looking at them, let us also examine our own hearts. With whom do you identify at this time in your life? Who offers you some insight and guidance about continuing to grow as a baptized disciple of Christ Jesus?

After you name and comment on each figure, pause and allow the listeners to reflect for a moment on the person whom you have named. Don't rush through the list!

John the Baptist: He lived, ate, and dressed like a hippie or "New Ager" and was out on the fringe of society, eating locusts and wild honey and wearing strange clothing made of animal skins. But he was able to articulate who he was, who Jesus was, and what his purpose in life was. He was clear about himself, his relationship with Jesus, and what he was called to do.

Mary: Her life was turned upside down. Her primary relationship was tested to the limit. She didn't appear to be doing things the way they should be done, and she questioned God. Because she prayed and pondered, she discovered that she could not only know God, but also bring God to birth in this world!

The Samaritan woman at the well: Her first reaction to Jesus reaching out to her and wanting to be in relationship with her was both attraction and skepticism. She needed lots of time to ask questions, to check out Jesus himself as well as what he was saying. She didn't get it at first, but once she realized who Jesus was, she immediately began her own ministry of spreading the word.

The man born blind: He needed to experience a real separation from his parents and community before he could see the possibilities of a new kind of life. Only through a gradual process did he learn to speak for himself and stand up to authority for what he knew to be true. He finally learned not only to trust his experience, but also to trust the person of Jesus.

The man with leprosy: He knew he wasn't very nice to be around, but, determined that he had nothing to lose, chose to risk being vulnerable. His vulnerability led him to Jesus, to healing, and to gratitude. He had the integrity to seek Jesus out in order to offer thanks, rather than going along with the crowd.

The friends of the paralyzed man: They knew that their friend couldn't get to Jesus alone. They found a way to help. They figured out a way to get in to Jesus, to talk to him, to ask him for what they needed, to bring their friend into personal contact with Jesus. They broke through both physical barriers and social norms to do the right and loving thing.

Nicodemus: He had a very hard time letting anyone know about his relationship with Jesus. But through his own introverted personality and reflective nature, and perhaps even because of a bit of humorous cynicism, he gave us one of the most beautiful discussions about baptism that has ever been recorded.

The woman with a hemorrhage of blood: Quietly courageous, gently assertive, unassumingly strong and brave, delightfully creative and wise, she knew that she should "stay in her place." Instead, she took a risk and made a decision to reach out, to get close, to touch. And she drew power from Jesus through her own power as a woman.

The rich young man: He was drawn to Jesus, curious and interested in what Jesus had to say about the meaning of life. He was educated and intelligent. He asked questions and gave good and right answers to Jesus' questions. And he went away sad because he still had some personal issues with which to wrestle.

Zacchaeus: He was less than honest with other people's money. He made a fool of himself in public by climbing trees simply because he wanted to sneak a look at Jesus without getting involved. And then he found that he was taken very seriously by Jesus, who engaged him in a challenging conversation. Zacchaeus was invited to open his heart and home, and Jesus broke bread with him at his table.

Mary Magdalene: She loved Jesus very much. She was faithful to him with all her heart. She just wanted to be close to him, but Jesus told her not to cling. He sent her off to his disciples, calling her to be the first to proclaim the good news of the Resurrection. She was compelled to leave her comfort zone and give herself to living and preaching the gospel.

Paul: He was so dramatic! And God dealt so dramatically with him. He was eccentric, committed, and driven. And his life was turned upside down—not by being knocked off his horse, but by meeting Jesus.

There are so many more. Perhaps there is a scriptural figure—who has not yet been named—with whom you identify. During this reflection time, you are invited to choose one figure with whom to spend some time. Have a conversation with that person, sharing your story and asking for advice, guidance, counsel, and insight. In your journal you may wish to write out your dialogue. Or you may prefer to enter into an imaginative conversation and then write a summary of your insights and discoveries. Other options are to write a letter to your scripture companion telling your own story. Then write your companion's letter of response to you, or you may do some creative writing, creating your scripture companion's imagined autobiography.

This exercise is not intended to be a scripture study, but an opportunity to bring our imaginations to the stories and figures from the New Testament that offer us guidance, direction, and counsel for our own gospel living.

- What does this person help you understand about following Jesus more closely and living out your baptismal commitment more fully?

- What does this scripture companion say to you about your own unique relationship with God in Christ Jesus and in the Church?

Reflection and Journal Writing
(45 minutes)

Sharing
(30 minutes)

Invite the candidates to share about their dialogue with their scripture companions. Encourage them to focus on their discoveries about the meaning of their baptismal commitment and the way of life that they are called to live in relationship with God, in Christ Jesus, and in the Church.

As unobtrusively as possible, take brief notes about the companions chosen and a key point shared by each candidate. These will be used in the concluding ritual.

Concluding Ritual
(15–30 minutes)

The concluding ritual flows directly and gently from the scripture companion sharing. Invite the participants to think about all that they have heard from each other and to call to mind the scripture companions who have been brought to life in each other's stories. Ask them to reflect on the longing for life and goodness and holiness that is common to all even in the midst of the variety and diversity among them.

Song

Invite the participants to sing an appropriate song about desire, longing, or anticipation.

Litany

Using the notes you took, pray a litany that names each person's scripture companion and one intercession based on the candidate's sharing. For example, if a person chose John the Baptist and shared an insight about being non-judgmental about a person's appearance, race, or lifestyle, your prayer might be, "John the Baptist, be our companion as we learn to accept others, regardless of their appearance, race, or lifestyle."

Invite the group to respond to each intercession by singing a short acclamation.

If the retreat is being held during Lent, conclude by reciting the Lord's Prayer together followed by an exchange of the sign of peace.

If the retreat is being held during a season other than Lent, call each candidate by name, saying,

"_____, you have been enlightened by Christ. Do you recommit yourself to living in the light of the grace of your baptism?

Response (allow the candidate to respond in her or his own words).

With a gesture, invite the candidate to light a taper and to form a circle as each person is called forward. After each candle is lighted, bless the candidate, saying,

"_____, may you walk always as a child of the Light supported by companions in faith."

Together, recite the Lord's Prayer, extinguish the tapers, and conclude with a sign of peace.

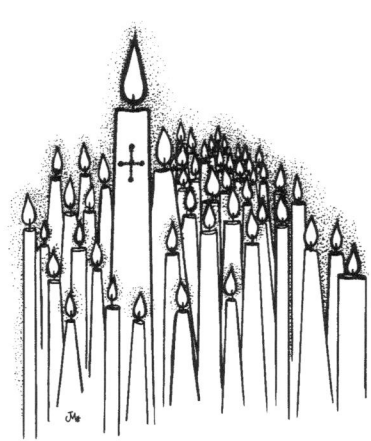

Retreat with the Woman at the Well

The Context

This three-hour retreat is designed for candidates who have had experience within the parish community and are seeking full incorporation into the sacramental life of the Church. It is expected that they have already been catechized—a catechesis that has led them to an understanding and appreciation for the gift of their baptism with its blessings, challenges, and responsibilities.

It is important that the director of Christian Initiation remember and celebrate the distinction between the candidates (baptized persons) and the catechumens (persons seeking baptism) throughout the process of initiation. This distinction should be maintained in both catechesis and liturgical celebration. Catechized candidates are to be received into full communion as soon as they are ready. This retreat could be helpful in the discernment process for candidates.

The optimum time for this retreat is either during Lent or any time prior to the candidates' first celebration of the sacrament of reconciliation, which is celebrated before reception into full communion with the Church.

Word of God

John 4:4–42. The foundation of this retreat is the magnificent passage from the Gospel according to John that tells the story of the woman from Samaria. It is one of the three primary "conversion Gospels" from the readings of Lent, Year A, proclaimed during the celebration of the first scrutiny. This passage from John's Gospel is well suited to a retreat for candidates because it highlights the movements of conversion that are familiar to all whose lives are affected by meeting Jesus at the water. The image of Jesus entering into conversation with the woman at the well offers the candidate a "mirror" in which to reflect on her or his journey of discipleship.

The Gospel is to be proclaimed as written and the reflection that follows is a first-person narrative in the imagined words of the Samaritan woman. It is important that whoever takes the role of the woman prepare well and be comfortable with the contemporary, colloquial interpretation.

Sacred Space

If possible, create a "well" around which to gather the group. Use a bucket of water (an empty bucket if the retreat is held during Lent) and some fabric and plants to enhance the beauty of the focal point. Place a chair or bench near the "well" in anticipation of a visit from the Samaritan woman, who will reflect on her experience of meeting Jesus there. Near the bucket, place the Book of the Gospels open to the Gospel of the Third Sunday of Lent, Year A.

 **LIVING RITE**

Prior to the retreat, invite each candidate to bring a small container of water from home or a favorite place. This will be used in the gathering rite of the retreat.

If the retreat is held during Lent, it is not appropriate to use water. Use the alternate choices in the gathering rite. At the end of the retreat, enhance the anticipation of the Easter renewal of baptismal promises by using an empty bucket and celebrating the final blessing without a sprinkling rite.

The rituals are very simple, calling forth the experience and response of the candidates. The retreat is designed as a seamless experience of the various elements: gathering, reflection, input, and ritual.

GATHERING
(20 minutes)

The leader welcomes the candidates and invites them to gather around the "well" accompanied by quiet, reflective music. There are many CDs available featuring music accompanied by sounds from nature; select a piece using water sounds.

Leader *(in these or similar words)*:

Water . . .

Water is all around us . . . and inside us.

Throughout time, we have used water to wash clothes, to grow flowers, to bathe our babies, to quench thirst, to celebrate sacred times in our lives.

Free-flowing water can be as light as the trickle of a stream, as peaceful as a meandering river, or have the depth and force of strong ocean currents or magnificent waterfalls.

The power of water can destroy—as death apparently does—making all things ready once again for new and unimagined life.

Women have a special relationship with the water through their cycle as it relates to the moon and the tides, the movement of water over all the earth.

Our journeys are as unique as the waters of the earth and, like those waters, we are forever changing.

Let us bless this water and let the images of water flow around us and through us.

(Alternate: Let us bless this gathering as we let images of water flow around us and through us.)

Let us bring the waters from our own river of life, and blend them with the waters of this wellspring.

(Alternate: Let us be grateful for the gift of water.)

Let us bring our thirst for the waters of life.

I invite each of you to come forward and say something about yourself and what image of water reflects who you are and how you are today: calm, raging, rippling, dry?

Come and bless the water with your own touch, blending the waters you brought from your own life with the waters of life we will share today.

(Alternate: Come and stand beside the well, knowing that soon the waters of life will be poured upon you once again as the Church celebrates the great paschal feast of Easter.)

HYMN

After each person shares, sing a hymn that has a water theme.

Prayer

Leader:
Let us pray.
God of flowing stream and still waters,
you are the source of all that we have and are.
We quiet ourselves and open our hearts to you,
waiting in joyful hope, knowing that you are here.

Reflection

Retreat is a time of waiting and expectation, of looking to the fulfillment of our hopes and desires. It is a way of being in life when we wait in joyful hope for the coming of our Savior, Jesus Christ—not only in the life to come, but in our real every-day life. It is an opportunity to share our struggles, to make sense out of life when things get turned upside down and we are confronted with the challenges of being a follower of Jesus. During retreat, as in all our prayer time, we can identify with those who question God. We can understand those who try to explain to a friend, spouse, or family member why and how things are happening in their lives and then are dismissed as not being believable. We can identify with moments of truth, of surrendering and letting go—at least for little pieces of time—and allowing ourselves to be touched and transformed by God who meets us where we are.

We are looking forward with joyful hope to your day of renewal and rebirth, the day when you will stand before the Church and say "yes" again to the waters of your own baptism. You have been accompanied throughout your life by many "water bearers." Certain special people have gone before you and have taught you that the wellsprings of life are deep within you. In order for the holy to be born in us and in our world, we must remember the people of faith who have gone before us and have taught us to come out of the shadows and into the light. We must remember the people who have been water bearers for us and who have taught us that the wellsprings of life are found when we are in right relationship with ourselves, with God, and with the people in our lives.

I invite you to reflect and write in your journal about a person who has been a water bearer in your life. What has that person taught you about the wellsprings of life that are yours through baptism?

Journal Reflection
(20 minutes)

- Name a person who has been a water bearer in your life.
- What has that person taught you about the wellsprings of life as a baptized Christian?

Dialogue
(20 minutes)
Invite each candidate to partner with another candidate to share what each has written in his or her journal.

Break
(15 minutes)

INTRODUCTION TO GOSPEL PROCLAMATION

Leader *(in these or similar words):*

Today we shall remember a woman—a water bearer.

She moves—not without struggle and a lot of questions—from simply drawing water at the well to discovering the waters of life bubbling up within her. She becomes not only a water bearer, but a bearer of good news for others.

We are invited to hear her story and allow it to be a mirror for our own baptismal journey. Where do you see yourself in the story? What does the story say to you? How does it challenge you? What does it call forth from you?

PROCLAMATION OF JOHN 4:5–42

Sing a simple Gospel acclamation as the leader approaches the Book of the Gospels and raises it up.

SILENT REFLECTION

Invite the candidates to reflect in silence and then write their responses to the following questions in their journals:

- Water is a powerful and life-giving resource in our life. What are some experiences in your life when water was very important?

- Often when we think of water, we think of thirst. What are some of the good and life-giving things in life for which you thirst . . . for which your family thirsts . . . for which the world thirsts?

- How do you know in your own life that you are drinking the waters of life and love? How do you know when you have turned away from the waters of life?

- When you think about the way we live as a community . . . as a nation . . . as a world . . . what are the things that keep everyone from being able to enjoy the waters of life? What is *one* thing that you will do in the next week to make someone less "thirsty" for good things in life or for love?

DIALOGUE

Invite the candidates to share their reflections. If the group is larger than eight people, divide into smaller groups.

BREAK
(10 minutes)

THE VISIT
(15 minutes)

The leader or someone else should be prepared to assume the role of a visitor to the group, assuming the persona of the Samaritan woman. She may wear a simple scarf around her head, walk in bare feet or sandals, and carry a bucket or jar of water. Once seated at the chair or bench near the "well" in the center of the room, she addresses the group in a conversational tone in these or similar words, as if telling her own personal story. If reading the script, she should make frequent eye contact with the candidates, speak slowly and clearly, and use various tones of voice to express the affective meaning of the words.

It had been a hot and busy day. I had to go to the well to draw water.

I never went when the other women did; it was too hard. For a while I tried, but I got sick and tired of their gossip about me, and of all the things they said behind my back. They thought it was behind my back, anyway! I could hear their body language louder than any voice. And it wasn't very nice. They thought they knew about me. They thought I was a bad woman. They thought they knew what was going on, that they knew the real story and they had no problem passing it around, never mind whether or not it was true.

So this time I went to the well at noon. It was hot and bright outside, and no one else would want to go at that time to carry a heavy water jar. Something about going out into that light made me feel alive and free. I even had a deep-down feeling of excitement or expectation.

What a surprise when this stranger showed up as I was drawing out the water. He was a Jew. I couldn't believe that! A Jew, right there at our well. And then he asked me for some water. No way! I'm supposed to give him water? I thought maybe he was making fun of me. No Jew would ask a Samaritan for water. Besides, it was outrageous that he'd ask me, a woman and in public? Not a chance.

But that's exactly what happened. He asked me for water. I confronted him right then and there. I asked him how he could be breaking all the rules by talking to me. He gave me a very strange response. He told me that if I knew who he was, I would ask him for water . . . living water. Water so I'd never be thirsty.

So I did. I asked him to give me some water because I was very tired of trekking out to the well and back, and if he had some magic water that would satisfy me, I could quit the daily trip to the well. I couldn't figure him out, but he intrigued me so I stayed with him a while longer. "Give me some of your living water, Sir," I said.

That's when it happened. He started talking to me like a real person. He treated me as if he knew me and even as if he liked me. He started a conversation as if we were two adult friends who had something to discuss, not like he was putting me down for being a woman or being from the wrong side of town. The first thing he said was that I should go and call my husband. Right away I knew that something very important was going on. You see, I don't have a husband.

He must have figured that out. He also knew that I had already had five husbands. Five stories. Five lives. Five attempts to center my life on someone or something that would last. Five tries at loving and living well. And this last try wasn't working either. I never felt as though he were worried about all the particulars or broken rules. I just knew that he was telling me that there was a way I could give my life to someone and be fulfilled. Now all his talk about living water was starting to make some sense!

I could see that he was more than just some nice guy. Maybe he was a prophet. He surely could see the signs of what was going on in my life. And he knew what needed to be challenged and changed if I was ever going to be filled with love and life. He called it living water.

So I decided to ask him some more questions. I decided I'd challenge him a bit and ask him to explain all about worship. If he was really a prophet, he ought to be able to explain to me about the conflict people had about the right way to worship and the right place to worship. He could tell me the right answer once and for all. But his answer was amazing! He said that it isn't the rules that matter, not even the place or way someone worships.

He said that true worship is about being in relationship with God in spirit and in truth. That made a lot of sense to me. I knew in my heart how the truth made me free and how my spirit just lifted up to God in praise and thanks, even when I had to face the fact that I'd made some pretty bad decisions in my life.

It occurred to me that I'd heard about a messiah that was to come. He was someone who was going to teach us everything we needed to know. I was beginning to learn through my conversation with this man what I needed to know—he was the person on whom I could center my life. Through him, with him, and in him, I could find a relationship that would last. With him I could live and love well. With him, I would be fulfilled at last. He could be my living water! So when he told me that he was the Messiah, of course I believed him.

When that happened I just had to share it with someone. The first thing I did was go straight back into the town where all those people were and told them to come see someone who really knew me and understood me and everything I'd ever done. Just as I was leaving the well, several men who had been traveling with my new friend came and caught us having a conversation. They didn't ask anything about it; they just looked at me and at him with a very strange look. He really wasn't supposed to be talking to a woman. I found out later that they thought he'd lost his senses and that maybe he needed something to eat. But he started talking about food in the same way that he talked about water—sort of poetically, as if food and water were symbols of something else more important. They didn't seem to understand even though he kept telling them he had some really good food and that he was satisfied just knowing that he was doing God's work.

I left the well and ran back to the town to tell my story. I left my water jar behind. Somehow, the regular routine of my life didn't seem so important any more. I told everyone I could about what had happened to me, and they came around themselves to find out more. They were very impressed and even asked him to stay for a couple of days. Imagine a Jew staying in our Samaritan town!

I knew that in our little town there were a lot of thirsty people who needed to know that they could be filled up with living water if only they could meet someone like him. I knew there could be a lot of changes in the way we treated one another if we listened to him and lived in spirit and truth the way he talked about.

After a couple of days, a lot of those people came back to me. They told me they believed for themselves now, not just because I had told them my story. My mission was accomplished. I felt fulfilled because now the living water was being shared among all of us. In our town, that made all the difference!

REFLECTION
(25 minutes)

Invite the candidates to think about what the visitor has shared with them.

Ask them to respond to the following journal questions and write their own prayer of renewal in their journals.

- What is your response to the visit from the Samaritan woman?

- What is your prayer for yourself as you look forward to renewing your own baptism and encountering again the living waters of baptism?

- What are you willing to tell "the whole town" about your encounter with Jesus and the living waters of baptism in your own life?

Concluding Ritual
(20 minutes)

Invite each candidate to come to the "well" and to share her or his prayer. After each person shares, invite the group to hold this person silently in prayer.

Leader:
Go forth and allow the living waters to bubble up within you.
As you use water during the next days and weeks, receive its gifts. Allow water to call you, challenge you, and comfort you as you continue your journey of faith.

Invite candidates to bless one another with water.
(Alternate: Invite candidates to share a sign of peace.)

Hymn
Conclude with an appropriate hymn.

Chapter Five
Purification and Enlightenment

In its fullness,
the rose knows the paradox
of beauty and pain.
Secure in the ground of its being,
the rose brings forth full bloom
on thorny stem.
Symbol of passion,
the rose blooms as memory
of love and suffering,
promise of forgiveness and fidelity,
and image of everlasting life.
Enter the rose!

PERIOD OF PURIFICATION AND ENLIGHTENMENT

The Period of Purification and Enlightenment coincides with the liturgical season of Lent. It is a time of intense preparation for the celebration of Easter and the sacraments of initiation. For the elect, it is a time of spiritual retreat and reflection in anticipation of the continuation of their faith journey through the waters of baptism to the eucharistic life of the fully initiated. For the baptized members of the assembly, it is a time of renewal and recommitment to the promises made at baptism.

Three rites of scrutiny are celebrated during Lent. At each one, the Church prays for and with the elect that they may be freed from sin and purified and strengthened as they approach the sacraments of initiation. "The scrutinies are meant to uncover, then heal all that is weak, defective, or sinful in the hearts of the elect; to bring out, then strengthen all that is upright, strong, and good. For the scrutinies are celebrated in order to deliver the elect from the power of sin and Satan, to protect them against temptation, and to give them strength in Christ, who is the way, the truth, and the life" (¶141 RCIA). At the conclusion of each scrutiny a prayer of exorcism is said over the elect.

The scrutinies take place within the ritual Masses of Christian initiation on the Third, Fourth, and Fifth Sundays of Lent. The readings prescribed for these Sundays are from John's Gospel, proclaimed in Year A: the Gospel of the Samaritan woman at the well, the Gospel of the healing of the man born blind, and the Gospel of the raising of Lazarus. When the scrutinies are celebrated—even in Years B and C—the Year A readings are used on the Third, Fourth, and Fifth Sundays of Lent. These are the "premier" conversion Gospels, each one a paradigm of the conversion process for all believers.

Candidates who have been called to continuing conversion and/or are preparing for full initiation into the Catholic Church through profession of faith, confirmation and Eucharist, do not participate in the scrutinies. The scrutinies are rites for the unbaptized. The twilight retreats in this section are intended primarily for the elect. However, candidates, godparents, and sponsors may benefit from participation in them with the purpose of renewing their baptismal commitment rather than preparing for a rite of scrutiny. Their presence may offer support and encouragement to the elect, particularly if there are very few elect in the group. In mixed groups, it is important for the leader to maintain clear distinctions between the baptized and unbaptized throughout the Lenten season.

Two retreats in this section are designed as preparation for the celebration of the scrutinies. The scrutiny ritual is outlined in the *Rite of Christian Initiation of Adults* and includes many options for adaptation to local circumstances of persons, time, and place. It is strongly recommended that the intercessions for each scrutiny reflect the articulated concerns and desires of the elect, the signs of the times, and the needs of the community and the world at large. By facilitating and listening well during the twilight retreats, the leader will be able to craft a litany of intercessions that echoes the life and reality of the particular community gathered to celebrate the scrutiny. This will contribute a great deal to a rich and profound experience of the scrutinies for the elect and for the gathered assembly.

There are two twilight retreats in this section, one for the first scrutiny and one for the second scrutiny. The retreat leader or catechumenate director can prepare a twilight retreat in preparation for the third scrutiny using one of these as a model. This section also includes a retreat for Holy Saturday morning that incorporates the preparation rites prescribed by the *Rite of Christian Initiation of Adults*.

Twilight Retreat: The First Scrutiny

The Context
The first scrutiny of the elect is celebrated on the Third Sunday of Lent. This two-hour twilight retreat is designed as preparation for the scrutiny. Participants in the retreat are the elect. Godparents, sponsors, and candidates for full initiation may be invited into the retreat experience with the understanding that the primary intent of the retreat is the preparation of the elect for the scrutiny to be celebrated on Sunday. The retreat should be held during the week prior to the first scrutiny, preferably in the evening. The retreat experience could be enhanced for smaller groups if the elect from nearby parishes were invited to participate.

Word of God
According to the Ritual Masses for Christian Initiation, found in the *Roman Missal*, the Liturgy of the Word for the Third Sunday of Lent, Year A, is celebrated for the first scrutiny. The Gospel story of the Samaritan woman and Jesus' promise of living water will be the source of reflection for this twilight retreat. Its profound and rich imagery will draw the elect into a deeper understanding of their own process of conversion and the promise of living water, which they will receive through baptism. A suggested reflection on the Gospel is provided for the leader. It serves as an invitation to the elect to examine their own lives as the Spirit scrutinizes their hearts in anticipation of the ritual celebration.

Sacred Space
The environment should be simple, even stark, in the spirit of Lent. Use Lenten purple fabric and such things as dry branches, cactus, and rocks to create a focal point that is pleasing, but not elaborate. Water should not be used. This is the season of dryness, thirst, and anticipation of the living water. An empty bucket or water jar may add to the environment. Place the scripture or Book of the Gospels, open to the fourth chapter of the Gospel of John, at the center of the focal point. Provide a book of the scripture for each of the elect.

Living Rite
Because this retreat is preparatory to the celebration of a significant rite, there is little ritual action within the context of the retreat itself. As presider over an evening of prayer, the leader is responsible for creating a reflective, reverent atmosphere appropriate to the season and the content of the retreat reflections. The solemnity of the evening depends largely on the leader's own preparation and style.

Most importantly, the leader needs to listen well to the reflections of the elect throughout the evening and perhaps take notes on what is shared. The intercessions for the rite of scrutiny (¶153 RCIA) may (and ideally should) be rewritten to reflect the reality of the particular group, circumstances, time, and place. They should echo the issues and concerns shared by the elect during this retreat. As the assembly's plea to God for purification and enlightenment for the elect, the response to the intercessions during the scrutiny may be sung.

GATHERING
(20 minutes)

Welcome the elect (and other participants) to the evening of retreat. Emphasize that this evening and the twilight retreats that will take place during the next two weeks are special opportunities for the elect to intensify their preparation for the Easter sacraments.

> **Include the following points in your introductory remarks:**
>
> Conversion is a process of both accepting God's gift of grace and new life and of acknowledging our own sinfulness as we respond to God's unconditional love. All participants are invited to enter into this evening as sacred time.
>
> On Sunday, the gathered assembly will pray for them during a special rite called the scrutiny.
>
> It is the Spirit of God who scrutinizes our hearts. As we reflect on both our sinfulness and our gifts, we are guided by God's Spirit of truth and love.
>
> This evening's retreat is an opportunity to prepare for the first scrutiny on Sunday by naming our thirst for God and our desire to receive the living water of baptism.

Invite the participants to gather into groups of three. Ask them to name as many "thirsts" as they can from their own experience. Give them some examples: thirst for water, thirst for beauty, thirst for love. Invite them to share their thirsts and to talk about what it feels like to experience thirst.

PROCLAMATION OF JOHN 4:5–42
(10 minutes)

An appropriate Lenten Gospel acclamation may be sung.

REFLECTION
(10 minutes)

Leader *(in these or similar words)*:

This passage from the Gospel according to John is one of the richest and most profound in our scriptural tradition. It was written for a community of believers who realized that Jesus' return in glory was not imminent. They were, as we are, in it for the long haul. This was a community that needed to clarify and claim its identity and to make clear choices about its practices and how its members would live as followers of the risen Jesus. It is a Gospel full of poetic and inspirational imagery: light, darkness, thirst, bucket, fields, harvest, wheat, food, wellsprings, and living water. It is also a Gospel filled with paradoxes—things are not always as they appear. Who would ever have imagined that this woman of questionable reputation would end up being the first to evangelize a whole town and bring them to faith in Jesus!

The Church gives us this Gospel passage on the Third Sunday of Lent because of its power to touch us and lead us closer to the living water of baptism. It is a passion Gospel, not about the passion and death of Jesus, but about God's passionate love for each of us. It is about God's passionate desire for each of us to draw from the living water and to come into the fullness of our potential as human persons. We are meant to come into intimate relationship with God in Christ Jesus.

Andrew Lloyd Weber created the Broadway play, *Aspects of Love*, in which there is a beautiful song called "Love Changes Everything." Love changes everything, and that change is "conversion." Conversion is our lifetime journey, our ongoing project as people of faith. It is our focus in a particular way during this Lenten season, and it is what we are called to day after day.

What does the woman from Samaria teach us about conversion? What can we learn from her about our own journey of faith, our own conversion? Her story is our story, too.

We learn from her, first of all, that conversion is a process. It takes time. It doesn't happen in an instant. We move deeper and deeper into the wellsprings of God's love and revelation as we grow in faith. Notice that the woman initially recognized Jesus as simply a man, a Jew, who was passing through her town. Because she remained engaged in conversation with him, she realized that he was a holy man, and she called him a prophet. Pursuing her conversation and relationship with him, she finally was ready and able to recognize him as the Messiah. Her conversion took time, conversation, engagement, and finally a real relationship with Jesus that ultimately changed her life.

> What is my conversion story? How have I deepened my relationship with God in Christ and in the Church?

This woman of Samaria teaches us that conversion starts with God's initiative. It is not something we can do for ourselves or manage on our own. It is not something we can earn. God will meet us where we are and how we are, just as Jesus met the woman at the well. And, as she did, we simply need to respond. We need to be open to the signs of God's presence and action in our life and to stay engaged, even when the going gets tough.

> What is God initiating in my life now? Where am I and where is God meeting me?

From the woman at the well we learn that conversion is founded on truth. Notice that she came to the well at midday, at high noon, when the light was the brightest. This image of coming into God's presence reflects that, in the light of God's love, she was able to name and accept her own truth. "I have no husband." "You are right in saying, 'I have no husband'; for you have had five husbands." But this wasn't really about the men in her life. This was about her repeated attempts to find love in all the wrong places. Just as we do, she made poor choices in trying to live and love well, but in accepting that truth about herself she was liberated from all those burdens. She was then free to accept the better offer: life-giving water.

> What do I need to bring into the light and name? What does God want to liberate in me?

This Gospel makes it clear that conversion transcends law, rules, and norms. It is important to note that Jesus was not particularly concerned with laws or rules; in fact, he broke a few himself when he entered the Samaritan town and spoke with a woman. Remember, Jews had nothing to do with Samaritans. Jesus, however, broke through and beyond society's norms when he spoke with this woman. In doing so, he demonstrated that he simply would not tolerate structures that were unjust, exclusive, racist, or oppressive. He doesn't engage in the controversy regarding where and how people ought to worship. Rather, he calls his disciples and this woman to worship in spirit and in truth. Even when Jesus scrutinizes the woman, he neither judges nor condemns. Her response is not one of fear. She is liberated, free, open, and energized to share her story. The scrutiny is simply a step along the way to becoming all that she was meant to be. It was part of the encounter that led her to the living water.

> Jesus neither judges nor condemns; what about me? What structures or societal norms am I called to confront? How is God calling me to work for change?

Finally, we learn from this woman of Samaria that conversion leads to action. The living water is not given to her alone. The waters of baptism are not for us alone. We must go forth and do as this woman did: make a difference in our town.

> To what action am I called? What story must I tell? What does my town, my community need from me?

If our initiation is to mean anything at all, if our encounter with Jesus in the sacraments of initiation is as real as that of the woman at the well, it will show forth in what we say and do and how we are in our town. What is it that will enable each of us to go forth from the font and table and, as the woman of Samaria did, share the living water with others? For what do I thirst? From what do I need to be freed? With confidence, let us name our thirst for living water and come into the light of God's love. Love changes everything.

REFLECTION
(30 minutes)

Invite the elect to take some time in quiet prayer and reflection with the woman of Samaria. Ask them to reread the Gospel in silence and, when they are ready, to write in their journals their response to the following:

- For what do I thirst? From what do I need to be liberated? What will enable me to go forth from the font of baptism and the table of Eucharist and, like the woman of Samaria, share the living water with others?

SHARING
(40 minutes)

The invitation to share responses from the journals should be offered in a prayerful, reverent manner. The atmosphere of recollection and reflection should prevail so that this does not become a time of discussion. Remind the elect that each person is sharing part of her or his sacred story, and we are gathered as a community of support and encouragement during this time of intense preparation for the Easter sacraments. Let them know that naming their truth may be difficult, that they are the custodians of their own story and truth, and that they are invited to share whatever they feel is appropriate and helpful to their Lenten journey of conversion.

After each person has shared, invite the group to take a moment of silence to reverence that person and to pray that the living water will flow into her or his heart. End the time of silence for each person with these or similar words:

Leader:
"_____, may your thirst be quenched.
May your cup be filled.
May your heart overflow with living water."

DISMISSAL
(10 minutes)

Prior to sending the elect forth, invite them to spend time each day until Sunday reflecting on the following questions in their journal and writing their responses as preparation for the celebration of the first scrutiny:

- What is my conversion story? How have I deepened my relationship with God in Christ and in the Church?

- What is God initiating in my life now? Where am I and where is God meeting me?

- What do I need to bring into the light and name? What does God want to liberate in me?

- Jesus neither judges nor condemns; what about me? What structures or societal norms am I called to confront? How is God calling me to work for change?

- To what action am I called? What story must I tell? What does my town, my community need from me?

Leader:
Invite the elect to kneel.

You may wish to play instrumental music or an appropriate hymn. Place your hands on the head of each of the elect, praying for her or him in silence.

Conclude with the words: "Let us stand and go now in peace."

Allow the end of the retreat to remain solemn. It is not necessary to provide refreshments or social time.

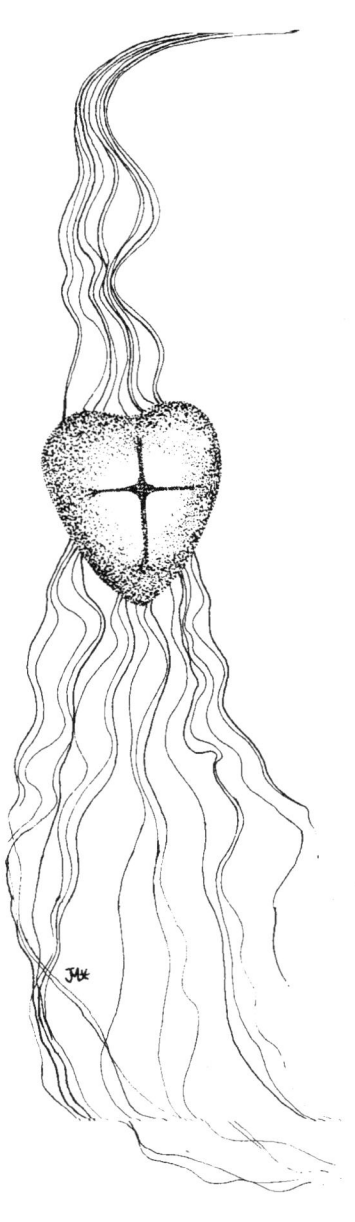

Twilight Retreat: The Second Scrutiny

The Context
The second scrutiny of the elect is celebrated on the Fourth Sunday of Lent. This two-hour twilight retreat is designed as preparation for the scrutiny. Participants in the retreat are the elect, together with their godparents and sponsors. Although they do not participate in the scrutiny, candidates may be invited to participate in the retreat as part of their Lenten preparation for celebrating the Easter mysteries. The retreat should be held during the week prior to the second scrutiny, preferably during an evening session.

Word of God
According to the Ritual Masses for Christian Initiation, found in the *Roman Missal*, the Liturgy of the Word for the Fourth Sunday of Lent, Year A, is celebrated for the second scrutiny. The Gospel story of the man born blind will be the source of reflection for this twilight retreat. The elect will be drawn into the imagery of darkness and light, blindness and sight. They will be invited to reflect on the blindness in their own lives, their need for healing, and the power of the light of Christ in their lives. Their identification with the movement from blindness to sight as part of their own conversion process will prepare them more fully to celebrate the second scrutiny. It will prepare them to receive the words of the Church addressed to them as they celebrate the sacraments of initiation: "You have been enlightened by Christ. Walk always as children of the light and keep the flame of faith alive in your hearts."

The familiar and enduring hymn "Amazing Grace" provides an introduction and context for the proclamation of the Gospel.

Sacred Space
The environment should be simple, even stark, in the spirit of Lent. Use Lenten purple fabric, adding such things as soil, rocks, or sand. Perhaps an old-fashioned lantern tipped on its side could be added. Do not use lighted candles, and keep the room dimly lit, particularly during the proclamation of the Gospel and the sharing time.

This is the season of darkness, to be lived through in anticipation of receiving the light of Christ. Place the scripture or Book of the Gospels, opened to the ninth chapter of the Gospel of John, at the center of the focal point. Provide a book of the scripture for each of the elect.

LIVING RITE

Because this retreat is preparatory to the celebration of a significant rite, there is little ritual action within the context of the retreat itself. As presider over an evening of prayer, the leader is responsible for creating a reflective, reverent atmosphere appropriate to the season and the content of the retreat reflections. The solemnity of the evening depends largely on the leader's own preparation and style. Most importantly, the leader needs to listen well to the reflections of the elect throughout the evening and perhaps to take notes on what is shared. The intercessions for the rite of scrutiny (¶167 RCIA) may (and ideally should) be rewritten to reflect the reality of the particular group, circumstances, time, and place. They should echo the issues and concerns shared by the elect during this retreat. The intercessions during the scrutiny, the assembly's plea to God for purification and enlightenment for the elect and themselves, may be sung.

GATHERING
(30 minutes)

Welcome the participants to this evening of retreat, reminding them that this is an important time of preparation for the sacraments of initiation. The Church will pray for and with them in a special way during the second scrutiny on Sunday.

Encourage the elect to share their feelings and thoughts about their experience of the first scrutiny.

Invite the participants to relax, listen, and open themselves to the movement of God's Spirit as you play an instrumental or choral version of the hymn "Amazing Grace."

Leader *(in these or similar words):*

The song that we just heard is one of the most familiar and beloved of our Christian tradition. It has been sung since 1748, the year in which it was written by John Newton. He experienced a profound conversion when the ship he was on was almost lost in a terrible storm at sea. He cried to God for deliverance, was saved from disaster, and then realized that God was indeed with him, delivering him all the time. He hadn't seen that before; now he saw it. And the song was born. It is interesting to note that, while the origin of the tune is not clear, it is commonly thought that it was a melody sung by slaves. Newton's poetic lyrics fit perfectly, and it became the song we know today.

A number of years ago, Bill Moyer produced a documentary entitled *Amazing Grace*, which explored the personal, familial, social, religious, and ritual use of the song. Passed down from generation to generation, "Amazing Grace" is heard everywhere from the grandest of cathedrals to the hollers of the Appalachians to the cotton fields of the Deep South. People of every denomination sing it at funerals, memorials, and significant community events. "Amazing Grace" is heard at most high-profile state and military funerals. What is its appeal? What is its universal truth that touches so many hearts? Listen to the words again:

> Amazing grace! How sweet the sound that saved a wretch like me!
> I once was lost, but now am found, was blind, but now I see.
> 'Twas grace that taught my heart to fear, and grace my fears relieved.
> How precious did that grace appear the hour I first believed.
> (Sublime gracia del Señor, que a un pecador salvó;
> fui ciego mas hoy miro yo perdido y el me amó.
> En los peligros o aflicción que yo he tenido aquí
> su gracia siempre me libró y me guiará feliz.)

Why do you think this hymn is so popular? Why does it touch so many people? Why is it sung over and over again?

Invite the participants to share what they think about the song. Listen for common themes and summarize them at the end of the sharing.

Continue in these or similar words.

We are all blind to something. Blindness is part of our common human experience. We are blind to the goodness in others. We are blind to opportunities to be generous and loving. We are blind to our own gifts. We are blind to our addictions. We are blind to God's revelation. Sometimes we are blind because we want to be, and we simply refuse to open our eyes and see. Sometimes we are blind because we have not yet been enlightened to see things or people as God would have us see them. And sometimes we are blind to the very presence and action of God in our own hearts and lives.

Much like us, there was a man who had an unexpected and miraculous encounter with Jesus. He had been blind from birth. Some people thought his blindness was punishment for his parents' sin. Although the man didn't know Jesus, Jesus healed him. This miraculous healing made a lot of people nervous. If Jesus was doing such things in their midst, they might have to accept him as the promised Messiah, the Christ. For the people of that town, accepting Jesus was clearly not the politically correct thing to do! To become a follower of Jesus meant giving up one's status. The power and practices of those who claimed to be men of God would be threatened. The way of life of teachers of the law and righteous, law-abiding citizens would be challenged. The only person who kept speaking his truth with conviction from his own experience was the healed man who had been born blind. In the end, he—the one who had been blind—was the one who could see most clearly. He came to see and acknowledge Jesus as the Son of Man, a name reserved only to the Savior. Those who thought they saw everything clearly were, in fact, truly blind because they refused to see the truth.

Gospel Proclamation and Reflection
(45 minutes)

Leader:
Let us listen to the Gospel proclamation and enter into the story of this blind person.

Invite the participants to remain seated, and being seated yourself, take up the scripture and proclaim the Gospel as the rich and wonderful story it is. Vary your tone of voice and feel free to use gestures to enhance the proclamation in order better to convey the text's meaning.

Proclamation of John 9:1–41

Reflection

At the end of the proclamation, ask the participants to share briefly with one other person:

- What particularly touched you or struck you as you listened to the Gospel?

Then invite the participants to share with their partners where they find themselves in the Gospel:

- With whom or with what part of the story do you most identify at this time?

After the pairs have shared their responses to the Gospel, invite the participants to reflect and respond to the following questions in their journals:

- What blindness am I aware of in my own life? Where do I need healing?

- What blindness in our community, town or city, society needs healing?

- How has the light of Christ touched my life?

SHARING
(40 minutes)

Invite the elect to share their responses to the journal questions. If there is time, invite the godparents, sponsors, and candidates to share aloud after the elect have had the opportunity to do so.

The invitation to share responses from the journals should be offered in a prayerful, reverent manner. The atmosphere of recollection and reflection should prevail so that this does not become a time of discussion. Remind the elect that each person is sharing part of her or his sacred story, and we are gathered as a community of support and encouragement during this time of intense preparation for the Easter sacraments. Let them know that naming their truth may be difficult, that they are the custodians of their own story and truth, and that they are invited to share whatever they feel is appropriate and helpful to their Lenten journey of conversion.

- With whom or with what part of the story do I most identify at this time is my faith journey?
- Where and in whom have I witnessed the Light of Christ shining?
- What is my light? What is my gift to the world as I approach the sacraments of initiation?
- Write a prayer or draw a symbol or picture about amazing grace in your life.

BLESSING AND DISMISSAL
(5 minutes)

At the end of the sharing, invite the elect to kneel and the other participants to gather around them, extending hands in prayer over them. Pray together in silence and then pray the following blessing aloud:

Leader:
As you continue your journey of faith,
may you be enlightened by Christ.
May you grow in wisdom and insight.
Healed by Christ Jesus, may you walk always as children of the light.
Throughout your life,
may you keep the flame of faith alive in your hearts.

Invite the elect to stand and conclude by singing the first two verses of "Amazing Grace."

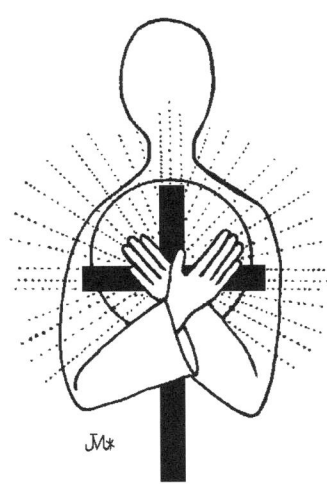

Holy Saturday Retreat and Preparation Rites

THE CONTEXT

The *Rite of Christian Initiation of Adults* calls for the elect to gather together on Holy Saturday in immediate preparation for the celebration of the sacraments of initiation at the Easter Vigil. The elect are encouraged to "refrain from their usual activities, spend their time in prayer and reflection, and, as far as they can, observe a fast" (¶185 RCIA).

Certain rites of preparation are prescribed, and "the choice and arrangement of these rites should be guided by what best suits the particular circumstances of the elect" (¶186 RCIA).

This retreat includes the Ephphetha rite, the recitation of the Creed, and an adaptation of the rite of choosing a baptismal name. The retreat should be adapted according to need in places where the presentation of the Creed has not yet taken place, where the presentation of the Lord's Prayer has not taken place, or where the choosing of a baptismal name is an appropriate addition. The retreat has four "modules" that can be adapted, interchanged, or used as the basis for creating a retreat suitable to particular groups and circumstances.

The retreat is designed so that it can be adapted to a very small group or even to one person preparing for initiation. Godparents, sponsors, parishioners, and candidates may be invited to be present in support of the elect who will be participating in the preparation rites.

The amount of time designated for each segment of the retreat will depend on the number of participants. Schedule the retreat with a break between each section, and time for reflection as appropriate. The retreat experience is meant to be unhurried, with a gentle, calm pace enhancing the ritual celebrations, reflection, and sharing.

The rites are exclusively for those who are preparing for baptism. If the group includes candidates completing initiation at the Easter Vigil, their preparation may be enhanced by participation in the scripture reflection, sharing, and common prayer that are part of the retreat experience.

WORD OF GOD

The scripture texts selected for this retreat are among those recommended in the *Rite of Christian Initiation of Adults*.

The first text, Isaiah 62:1–5, is about being called by name and is the centerpiece of the gathering experience for the retreat. If the rite of choosing a baptismal name is appropriate, it may be inserted after the gathering (¶200 RCIA).

The Ephphetha rite is preceded by the proclamation of Mark 7:31–37, a passage that tells of the deaf-mute person whose ears were opened by Jesus' command, "Ephphetha!"

The recitation of the Creed takes place after the reading of Matthew 16:13–17 and a reflection on Jesus' question to the disciples, "But who do you say that I am?"

Each of these selections draws the elect to see their own stories in the word of God proclaimed and lived among them as they prepare to enter the waters of baptism. The retreat design also offers them the opportunity to reflect on a scripture passage of particular significance to them at this moment in their journey of faith.

Sacred Space

The best place to experience this retreat is somewhere quiet, preferably away from the parish church. Ideally, arrangements would be made to gather at a retreat house, home, convent, or a small chapel. On Holy Saturday morning, the parish church is usually a place of too much activity to provide the atmosphere appropriate for prayer and reflection.

It is important to prepare the space without using the signs and symbols or decor that will be part of the initiation rites to be celebrated in the evening. Candles, water, bread and wine, oil, flowers, and other Easter decorations should be avoided. Instead, the sacred space should focus on the scripture or Book of the Gospels. An appropriate icon may be used. It might be effective to add something from the sacred space created for each of the scrutiny retreats, such as an empty water jar, a broken lantern, or linen cloths. The simplicity of the sacred space will serve to enhance the atmosphere of fasting and anticipation of what is yet to come.

Living Rite

The central rite in this retreat is the proclamation of the Word. It takes place several times throughout the retreat experience. How the leader handles the book containing the Word, proclaims it, and invites both silent and shared reflection on it can contribute significantly to the atmosphere of reverence, respect, and reflection.

It is of utmost importance that this gathering not be used as a time of rehearsal or instruction for the Easter Vigil. The presider, liturgical ministers, and godparents should be familiar with the order of worship and their responsibilities throughout the Vigil, and be prepared to guide the elect through their initiation. To rehearse with those to be initiated contributes to their anxiety about doing things "right" and can diminish the impact of the experience. Assure the elect that their godparents and the liturgical ministers will guide them through the celebration. In this way, they will be free to experience fully, in the moment, the sights, sounds, symbols, colors, words, textures, tastes, feelings, and discoveries that come from being immersed into the sacramental richness of the Easter Vigil celebration.

I. Gathering

Begin with a time for each person to share her or his feelings at this moment of anticipation. If the group has not gathered during Holy Week, take time to talk about the experiences of the week, and address any questions that may have arisen.

Invite the participants to quiet themselves, to enter into this time of retreat with open hearts and minds, and to trust that the Spirit of God will continue to guide them through this day and the sacramental celebrations this evening.

Encourage them to let go of any concerns or anxieties and to allow themselves to experience the love of God, the support of the community, and the action of the Spirit in their lives in all that they experience this day and evening.

Remind them that this time of preparation is bringing them closer to the full incorporation into the life and mission of the Church for which they have been longing.

Assure them that this is a special time of grace and peace for them.

Gathering Song

Begin with an appropriate song.

Opening Prayer

Leader *(with hands in the orans position):*
Let us pray.
Lord Jesus Christ,
you are the living water for which we yearn,
you are the light of the world, our hope and our life.
Gather us to you today and make us a holy people.
Through your Holy Spirit, guide our day and our ways.
May we be drawn more deeply into the mysteries of love
and salvation that we,
together with your whole Church,
will celebrate in faith this night.
We pray in your holy name, now and forever.
Amen.

Proclamation of Isaiah 62:1–5

Response

A sung version of Psalm 95 or 103 is appropriate.

Reflection

Leader *(in these or similar words)*:
God's call to each of us is both personal and intimate. Tonight each of you will be called by name as you are baptized into Christ. You will be made new. In silence and in the depths of our own hearts, let us simply listen to the voice of God calling us each by name.

After a few minutes of silence the leader continues addressing each of the elect (and, if appropriate, each person participating in the retreat) in these or similar words:

_____, you have been called by name.
You shall be called God's Delight, because your God rejoices in you!

Following the call and naming of each person, (or every three or four persons if the group is large) all sing a refrain such as "Blessed Be God" or say together:
"Blessed be God who calls you, ____, by name!"

It may be that for personal, cultural, or other reasons, some of the elect have chosen a new name for baptism. In these cases, the naming of the elect as described in ¶202 RCIA may take place at this time.

II. Ephphetha

Proclamation of Mark 7:31–37

An appropriate Lenten Gospel Acclamation is sung.

Reflection

Leader *(in these or similar words)*:

"Ephphetha!" And immediately the man's ears were opened.

We are looking forward not just to the celebration of the sacraments of initiation at the Easter Vigil tonight. We are looking forward to the rest of our lives. There are three aspects of this Gospel that can offer us particular guidance for our ongoing journey through the font, to the table, and to the rest of our days as fully initiated members of the Church.

Jesus, the Gospel says, took the man off by himself, away from the crowd, and then performed the miracle of healing. We know that the touch of Jesus is individual and personal for each one of us. But how important it is to remember how this man got to Jesus! It was through the community. The people brought him to Jesus. Our personal relationship with Jesus is always in the context of a community. We need each other today and will continue to need a community of faith to help us, to support us, to understand our frailties and impediments, and to guide us always back to the source of our healing and life. As a community of faith, we must pray for one another, work with each other, support one another, and come to the Lord together.

Secondly, notice how the miracle happened. Jesus put his finger into the man's ears. Jesus spat and touched his tongue. And Jesus groaned. The action of God in our lives is not something far away from us, in some otherworldly realm that is removed from the things, people, and experiences of everyday life. No, God touches us in the same way that other people touch us. To be aware of God's action in our life, we need to be deeply in touch with our own humanness, the rhythms of our own lives.

Jesus, the Son of God, chose to take on our humanness and then to make water and mud and lilies, tax collectors and prostitutes, lepers and widows, women and children, light and oil, bread and wine, the means through which we find communion with God. To live fully the miracle of our lives, we need to cultivate an awareness of sight, sound, touch, color, taste, and smell in order to discover the connections between daily life and the revelation of God in life and liturgy. We need to develop the sensitivity to see the world as a place where the human and divine are one, where the Incarnation, Passion, and Resurrection are all over the place. The true spirituality that will sustain us throughout our daily struggle to live gospel lives is a spirituality that is grounded in the belief that "The Word became flesh and lived among us" and that God will meet us in our humanity and desires to bring our humanity to its fullness in Christ.

Finally, notice that the healed man just had to tell anyone and everyone what had happened to him. He spoke plainly. He told his story. He shared his truth. But the reason he did this was so that the people could know about Jesus. The result was that the man's friends and neighbors exclaimed about Jesus, "He has done everything well; he even makes the deaf to hear and the mute to speak."

What a wondrous thing we look forward to, knowing that our community of faith indeed will be able to say because of each of you, "God has done all things well. God has brought you to our community. We have seen God's glory through the miracle of your lives, your presence, your faith, and your witness." God's miracle of healing the man who was deaf and could not speak clearly is the same miracle that God is working in and among us today.

EPHPHETHA RITE

The ordinary minister of this rite is a priest or a deacon. The minister touches both ears and the lips of each of the elect and says, "Ephphetha: that is, be opened, that you may profess the faith you hear, to the praise and glory of God" (¶199 RCIA).

If there is no priest or deacon present, this adaptation of the rite may be used:

Leader

Invite each of the elect to come forward. Make the sign of the cross on the ears and on the lips as you pray:

May you continue to hear the story of God in your own lives,
in the scripture, and in the Church.
May your ears be opened ✠ to receive the word of God
in the word proclaimed, explained, and lived in this community of faith.
May your lips be opened ✠ to proclaim the glory of God
in your own words of compassion, justice, truth, and love.

Follow the Ephphetha rite or adaptation with an appropriate song.

III. RECITATION OF THE CREED

PROCLAMATION OF MATTHEW 16:13–17

An appropriate Lenten Gospel Acclamation is sung.

REFLECTION

Leader *(in these or similar words)*:

"Who do you say that I am?" Tonight you will answer this question with your lives. As you enter the waters of baptism, you will die with Christ and rise with him to new life. As you are anointed with the oil of chrism, you will be confirmed and strengthened in your baptismal mission to proclaim the message of the gospel in all that you do, say, and are, from tonight through the rest of your life. As you share at the table of Eucharist, you will receive and become the Body of Christ, and be sent forth to do your part to bring about the reign of justice and peace to your sisters and brothers.

"Who do you say that I am?" Tonight you will say that Jesus Christ is all in all, your brother, your Savior, your life, the life of the world.

"Who do you say that I am?" Tonight you will be asked to profess your faith publicly. May the Lord open your lips and may your mouth proclaim God's praise. It is your duty and your privilege to join this community of faith in professing the Creed that has been entrusted to you. With one voice, you and the whole Church will proclaim what we profess, what we teach, and what we believe.

PRAYER

(¶195 RCIA)

Leader *(with hands outstretched)*:
Let us pray.
Lord, we pray to you for these elect,
who have now accepted for themselves
the loving purpose and the mysteries
that you revealed in the life of your Son.
As they profess their belief with their lips,
may they have faith in their hearts
and accomplish your will in their lives.
We ask this through Christ our Lord.
Amen.

And so, I ask you, the elect of God's Church, what do you believe?

The elect respond by reciting the Creed that was entrusted to them in the presentation of the Creed, either the Apostles' Creed or the Nicene Creed.

Hymn

An appropriate song may be sung.

IV. Scripture Sharing

Invite the elect (and, if you wish, the candidates, godparents, and sponsors) to reflect on the scripture passages and/or liturgical experiences that have been most significant for them during their journey of conversion. Ask them to spend some time thinking about what that passage or experience adds to their anticipation of the sacraments of initiation this evening. After some time for private reflection, encourage them to share their insights with the group. In large groups it may be necessary to divide into smaller circles for sharing.

Intercessions

Conclude the sharing with an invitation to prayer. Encourage those gathered to bring to prayer the needs of the world, the Church, the parish community, and those who will be initiated this evening. If the group is comfortable with shared prayer, do not structure this time of intercession; if necessary, guide it and invite each person to add her or his prayer. It may be helpful to respond as a group to each intercession with a common response such as "Lord, hear our prayer."

At the conclusion of the intercessions, the leader invites all to stand and pray with hands in the orans position.

Leader:
With confidence and gratitude,
let us join together in the prayer
that has been given to us by Jesus
and that we are privileged to say as his sisters and brothers:
Our Father . . .

Dismissal

Leader:
May the Spirit of God be with you until we gather again to celebrate the Paschal Mystery at our Easter Vigil.

Chapter Six
Mystagogy

The time of pruning has come.
The rose yields to its own mystery.
Its glorious beauty gives way
to the deeper mystery
of death and life.

The cycle begins again . . .
and again . . .
and again.

The rose becomes more rooted,
more beautiful,
more generative as it offers its seed
to bring forth new life.

Enter the rose!

MYSTAGOGY

Through sacramental initiation, the neophyte continues the journey of faith into the rest of life as a disciple of Jesus Christ. It takes a lifetime to deepen one's appreciation of the Paschal Mystery and to make meaning of one's life through, with, and in the risen Christ. Officially, the time for the period of postbaptismal catechesis or mystagogy lasts for one year. In reality, it never ends. "This is a time for the community and the neophytes together to grow in deepening their grasp of the paschal mystery and in making it part of their lives through meditation on the gospel, sharing in the eucharist, and doing the works of charity" (¶244 RCIA).

The formational process is meant to continue long past the Easter Vigil. Mystagogy is the time when neophytes learn by probing their experience of the sacraments and of the community. Liturgical catechesis will lead them more deeply into the mysteries of faith. Reflection on scripture, which has been a critical part of their catechumenal formation, continues, and neophytes are called to reflect also on their personal experiences of font, chrism, and table. Reflection on word and sacrament will draw them more deeply into the life and mission of the Church.

The retreats in this section are designed for the fully initiated. They are appropriate for recently initiated neophytes, and also for parish groups gathered for prayer, reflection, and renewal as the people of God.

The first retreat is an all-day retreat to be held at the beginning of Advent. It may be divided into segments and spread out over two or three weeks. The reflections move through the readings for each Sunday of Advent, culminating in a ritual of commitment to the Advent journey from darkness to light. This retreat is easily adaptable to various age groups or a family retreat experience.

The second retreat is a half-day "anniversary retreat" for neophytes designed to be held on or near Pentecost. It is also suitable for a parish community. The retreat includes a renewal of baptismal promises and a table gathering for a meal.

Advent Retreat for the Fully Initiated

The Context

The beginning of a new liturgical year is an appropriate time to gather together those who have been initiated in the past few years along with their sponsors and godparents. This retreat is designed to provide reflection, in the context of the Advent scriptures, on the experience of living one's baptismal call. It begins with the celebration of Morning Prayer, which includes a reflection on the reading that sets the focus for the day. The Advent theme of light weaves the retreat together through scripture, faith sharing, prayer, and ritual.

This retreat may also be used as a parish retreat. One suggestion is to work with the youth minister and catechetical director to adapt the retreat in an age-appropriate manner in order to provide a family day of retreat for the parish as a whole. The closing ritual could be celebrated in common.

This is planned as a six-hour retreat, including an hour-long meal break. It may be divided into two evening experiences, or otherwise adapted according to the needs and circumstances of the group.

Word of God

The reading from the First Letter of John speaks eloquently of the reality of the Incarnation—the revelation of God is manifested in what we have heard and seen and watched and touched. The light of God breaks through the darkness of the world of sin and death as God's very Word becomes one of us. The spirituality of the newly baptized—as of all the baptized—will be developed and nurtured to the extent that God's dwelling among us is recognized in the persons, places, and experiences of every-day life. Our deep human longing for light and life leads people of faith to discover the revelation of God—the extraordinary—in the midst of the ordinary.

Sacred Space

If possible, celebrate Morning Prayer, the afternoon reflection-presentation, and the closing ritual in a church or chapel. Keep the lighting in the room dim and use candles lavishly! Use another gathering space for journal writing and sharing.

The focal point in the gathering space may be simple; use the Book of the Gospels, open to the readings for the First Sunday of Advent, as the primary symbol. Surround the Book of the Gospels with the evergreens or holly branches of nature's season of winter and the blue-violet fabric of the liturgical season of Advent. If there is a large group, set up chairs in smaller circles of six.

Living Rite

The outline for Morning Prayer is provided here. Invite the parish liturgy committee and/or music ministers to assist in the selection of psalms and hymns familiar to your parish community. Be attentive to the appropriate use of various languages and cultural settings when selecting lyrics and music.

The presider for Morning Prayer should be familiar with the postures and gestures appropriate to the role. The other ministers should be well prepared. If possible, invite a parish cantor to lead the participants in the singing of the psalms. The closing ritual recalls and images the Rite of Baptism and the renewal of baptism at which each of the newly initiated received a candle. Provide tapers for each participant. It is important to allow plenty of time for the solemnity of this renewal to be experienced by each participant. The attitude, tone of voice, and demeanor of the presider is significant in setting that tone, particularly during the questions for commitment.

Morning Prayer
(40 minutes)

If possible, begin with a procession to the church or chapel. Process in silence accompanied by the sound of a drum, chime, or singing bowl until all are gathered in the chapel space.

Invitatory *(sung by presider)*
O Lord, open our lips.
And we shall proclaim your praise.

Morning Hymn
An appropriate hymn, which expresses the theme of light, is sung.
Presider is seated; all are seated.

Psalm 63
A familiar setting is sung.

Psalm Prayer
Presider *(with hands in the orans position)*:
Holy God, creator of light, enlighten our minds and hearts;
fill us with your Spirit of wisdom and love.
May we praise you in all that we do,
giving honor and glory to your name.
We ask this through Christ our Lord.
Amen.
Presider is seated.

Psalm 27
A familiar setting is sung.

Reading
1 John 1:1–5

Reflections

The presider or another person offers the reflections in these or similar words.

Today, as we gather for a time of retreat, we are invited to become fully aware of our emptiness, our need, and our incompleteness. We are invited to acknowledge and experience the restlessness, the void, and the hunger within us. To some extent, each of us lives in darkness. We encounter shadows in ourselves and in others. Something's not right. We need the light. Longing for light, we wait in the darkness.

Within each of us is that deep longing, and deep longing is painful and lonely. We may try to fill it ourselves with busy-ness, concerns, and worries. We may even try to fill it with very good things such as service, ministry, activity, charity, or good works. We long for the light, and to fill up that longing we try, perhaps without realizing it, to identify or create the light for ourselves and for others.

Today is a reminder that what we long for, the light that shines in the darkness, is God. Only in God is there no darkness at all. The very longing that we experience can motivate us and challenge us to keep looking, keep seeking, keep journeying toward the light.

And how do we do that? This morning's reading from the letter of John gives us direction. On what are we spending our time? What do we hear, want to hear, avoid hearing? What do we see, want to see, avoid seeing? What do we touch, want to touch, want to avoid touching? Where does our longing lead us in this world— a world filled with the darkness of terrorism, poverty, hunger, oppression, homelessness, violence, illness, and indignities of all kinds? In the darkness, I can avoid hearing, seeing, and touching these realities; they are so ugly, they demand so much from me, and I feel so helpless in the face of them. In the light, I cannot avoid them; I must touch and be touched and that can inconvenience me, scare me, or repulse me. In the light, I must recognize and realize that there are and have been great change points in our world: September 11, 2001 is one of them. What has happened and is happening to us and to our world is real.

Where does my longing lead me in this inner world of fear, struggle, loneliness, doubt, and desire? In the darkness, I can go from day to day and project to project and relationship to relationship without much trouble. In the light, I cannot avoid dealing with my own truth.

We must live into the answers to these questions if we are ever to live as credible baptized disciples of Christ Jesus. Our baptism calls us truly to proclaim by our lives that the Word is life and that in God there is no darkness at all.

The truth is that the light shines in the darkness; the light surrounds us and enfolds us. The light fills us. The light is illuminating our hearts and minds, our relationships, our choices, and our world. All we have to do is go there, be there, turn toward it, and accept it. At first, it may seem blinding or harsh as we come out of the darkness, but, with time, our darkness will be turned to light and our longing will be fulfilled. Then we will be able to proclaim credibly, in the words of the letter of John, what we have heard, seen, watched, and touched. Then, the Word who is light and life will truly be our story. God's story needs to be told through our own stories.

Today is a time for us to focus on the choices we have made, choices that demonstrate what we have seen, what we have heard, what we have watched and touched. It is a time to renew that awareness, consciousness, and self-discipline that each of us needs in order to develop, over time, an attitude of hearing, seeing, and touching that reveals the light to us and through us.

Our own conversion, our own immersion in the light, is an ongoing process during which the light becomes more and more a part of who we are, and our very lives become proclamations of the truth, revelations of the light.

Each day becomes an Advent, and Advent teaches us how to live each day. Longing for light, we wait in the darkness. What choices will we make? Will we turn towards the light? What are we willing to see, hear, watch and touch? For what are we waiting?

Gospel Canticle
Presider gestures for all to stand.
A familiar setting of the Canticle of Zechariah is sung.

Prayers of Intercession
(Response: God of Light, hear our prayer.)

For the Church throughout the world: may we be signs of joyful hope as we wait for the coming of our Savior, Jesus Christ, we pray.

For our world of conflict and violence: may we recognize the face of God dwelling among us and live as people of peace, we pray.

For people who are poor and oppressed, suffering and violated, alone and fearful: may they learn how loved they are through our acts of justice and charity, we pray.

For families, especially for children: may they be strengthened and supported in living together in love and peace, we pray.

For our loved ones who have died: may they rest in peace and bless us through their prayers and presence in the communion of saints, we pray.

The Lord's Prayer
Presider stands with hands in the orans position and invites:
Let us pray now together (in the language of your choice) the prayer that Jesus gave us. Our Father . . .

Concluding Prayer
Presider *(with hands in the orans position)*:
God of Light, God of Love,
bless your people this day.
May the light of justice and peace
shine through the darkness of oppression and hopelessness.
May we be people of light and truth.
Through our words, our actions, and our relationships,
may we proclaim Jesus as the Light of the World.
This we ask in the name of Jesus and through your Holy Spirit.
You are one God, forever and ever.
Amen.

Blessing
Presider *(with hands outstretched)*:
May God bless us and keep us.
May God's face shine upon us.
May God be gracious to us and give us light and peace.
Amen.

Sign of Peace
Presider:
Let us offer each other a sign of peace.

Individual Reflection
(30 minutes)

JOURNAL QUESTIONS:

- Where and why do I long for light? What is the darkness with which I struggle right now in my life?
- Where do I hear, see, and touch the light most profoundly in my own life?
- What "God-story" is being told through me at this time in what others hear, see, and receive from me?
- What is my own heartfelt prayer today—a prayer that tells of my own longing for the light of God in my life? For my loved ones? For our world?

BREAK
(20 minutes)

DIALOGUE
(30 minutes)

Invite the participants to share their responses with a small group. Remind them that this is not a discussion. It is an opportunity to hear one another's stories and celebrate the light of God in each person's experience.

LARGE GROUP SHARING
(20 minutes)

Invite the participants to share with the large group anything that they heard in their small groups that they think would benefit everyone. The purpose of this time is not to repeat the stories that have been shared in the small groups, but to raise up any significant insights that emerged from the dialogue.

MEAL BREAK
(1 hour)

REFLECTION-PRESENTATION
(20 minutes)

The leader presents a reflection on the scriptures of the four Sundays of Advent in these or similar words.

Our baptismal journey continues, and together with the whole Church we begin anew. Advent has come again. A new liturgical year begins. Once more we find ourselves starting over, anticipating that which we remember and celebrate, the coming of our Savior, Jesus Christ. Each Sunday of Advent calls us to live our baptism more fully, more faithfully as disciples of Jesus and members of the Church.

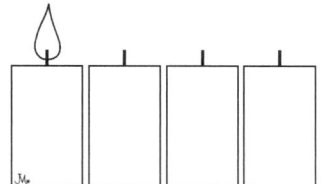

The message of the First Sunday of Advent is clear, direct, and simple. Stay awake! Be alert! September 11, 2001 made this message new and real in a profound way. You do not know when the Son of Man will come. You just don't know—you could be sitting at your desk, dropping your child off at day-care, keeping an appointment in a corporate office that you only occasionally visit. You just don't know. You could be on that one fateful plane trip; you could have kissed your spouse and children good-bye for the last time. You just don't know.

But the message of the First Sunday of Advent was not addressing the unknowns of terrorism and war, or of anthrax and bombs in unexpected times and places. It focused on being prepared at all times, at any time to recognize the face and presence of God in your life. What are we waiting for? We are waiting for God to burst into our lives in unexpected times and places, and we are called—even warned—to be ready!

What does this say to us about the pace of life we live? It takes a lot of time and energy to stay awake—to be aware and vigilant. As baptized disciples of the Lord we are called to see things differently and to hear things differently as we journey in this world. Listen to the ads today, to the political commentary that goes on non-stop, to the talk shows on radio and television, and notice the banners that demand your attention and response each time you go on line.

We are called to live Advent lives by thinking differently about what we hear and see—thinking differently from the acceptable and politically correct norms of our society. We are called to make an "all the time" commitment, to develop an attitude toward life and relationships that is aware, sensitive, compassionate, and responsive so that light and goodness can penetrate the darkness.

Our baptism calls us to find ways to be in the light and to invite others into the light. Often that light shines brightly in the variety of cultures, lifestyles, languages, and economic classes that characterize our communities, but we miss it because we are in the darkness of our own narrow vision and busy-ness about other things. Too often that light is missed because we expect things to be a certain way, and we do all we can to make it go that way and to keep things within our comfort zone.

The First Sunday of Advent gives us our wake-up call, and it is a call to let go of everything in order to be alert to everything. It is our responsibility to awaken ourselves to new approaches and other people's perspectives—or we may miss something! But we must wait and be ready. We just don't know when and how the opportunities to see and understand more will come: the chances to welcome the Lord into our midst in new and unimagined ways, the possibility of responding in personal and profound ways to the free gift of salvation. In the same way, we know neither the day nor the hour of our ultimate encounter with the light, which will come through the darkness of death. It will come.

The light shines on in the darkness. When it shines in the most unexpected of places and through the most unexpected of persons or circumstances, will we be awake, ready? How will we respond? Is our sense of expectation this Advent born of fear, or of a joyful hope as we wait for the coming of our Savior, Jesus Christ—today and every day until he comes again in glory?

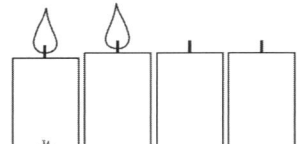

The Second Sunday of Advent fills our ears and hearts with the words of John the Baptizer: "Prepare the way of the Lord!" He's coming. Get ready—fill in the valleys, make the mountains and hills low. Straighten things out. Smooth things out. Make things even. Because all flesh shall see the saving power of God!

John was certainly aware of who he was and what his role was in the plan of salvation. He knew what he was there for and he made sure that others were clear about that, too. In like manner, we need to be aware of our own personal call and relationship with the Lord. We need to develop a strong sense of our discipleship. And we must not lose sight of the meaning and responsibility of our baptism. As John was, we need to be centered on the One who calls us into intimate relationship.

How important it is, then, for us to take the time to reflect on our own faith story. Who have been the ones who have prepared the way for me? What are the hills and valleys that have needed leveling in my life?

As disciples of the Lord Jesus, we must live, moment by moment, our own response to the covenant that was sealed between our loving God and us at baptism. What does it mean to each of us that baptism is not simply a water rite, but the true baptism in the Holy Spirit for which John told the world to get ready?

The readings of the Second Sunday of Advent also herald a strong call for us to act with justice. Certain mountains in our society need to be leveled: mountains of money and materialism; mountains of arrogance and anger; mountains of classism, racism, and sexism. There are mountains of terrorism and fear; mountains that separate classes of people and prevent access to food, home, education, and health care; mountains which separate East from West, Muslim from Christian. There are mountains too high for the "little ones" of society—poor people, women and children, mentally ill and physically sick people, refugees and aliens—to surmount alone. Who will traverse the way with them? Who will make it possible for them to get to the other side of their life challenges? How does our baptism call us to help bring down these mountains, and how do we call our sisters and brothers in faith to join us in this work?

There are valleys to be filled in: hollow and distended stomachs; pits of depression and despair; graves of victims of violence and capital punishment; valleys and villages of abandoned, poor, and elderly people and children without hope; depressions where towers of steel and hope, bustling with life, have fallen. With what do we attempt to fill in these valleys? What do we, the Church, contribute as we struggle toward making things more level, more just? There are crooked things in our communities and cities and churches to be made straight.

When and where do we choose to bend one way or another? How do we make those decisions? There are rough things to be made smooth. How do we reconcile and heal, and at the same time challenge, chafe, and rub away the roughness and toughness that interfere with just and right relationships with people and within systems? How much does the call to justice inform and inspire our participation in the life and mission of the Church?

On the Third Sunday of Advent, John continues his urgent message. "He's coming. I'm not the one on whom you should be focusing. Look around at what is going on! I am just the voice calling your attention to him and his action in the world. Go and tell what you hear and see: the blind see, the lame walk. You think I'm important for what I do, but I just baptize with water. He's coming and he will baptize you with the Holy Spirit. He is so much greater than I! I'm not worthy even to tie his shoe! Get ready; you don't want to miss him! Actually, he's right here in the midst of you. Don't miss him!"

John's urgency must have been contagious. Is yours? What keeps you going? What do others see and hear from you that make them want to know your God? What voice do you speak? Do you really have an urgent message worth spending your life on?

At baptism we were called God's dearly beloved. We were given a share in the mission of Jesus through the Church.

As John was, we need to be clear about who we are and what our message is. This calls for humility and truth, confidence that we have been called and chosen, and conviction that God is the center of our lives. Each of us, in our own way, has the task and privilege of preparing the way of the Lord in our midst by our words and by the way we live our lives. Each of us has to get out of the way in order to point the way to a God whose tenderness and compassion are so much greater than our own.

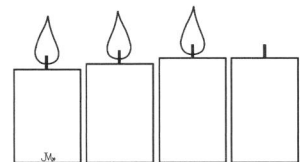

Finally, we come to the Fourth Sunday of Advent. "Joseph, don't be afraid to marry Mary! She's pregnant, yes. But she will have a son and name him Emmanuel, God-with-Us. Can you believe that?"

"Hello! You are so full of grace. Blessed are you and blessed is the child you carry within you! Let it be done according to God's word!"

What a mess things were: a pregnant bride, a hurt and confused fiancé, angels carrying messages, a menopausal woman about to give birth! Here was plenty of good material for gossip, judgment, fear, and doubt. Here were more than enough reasons to believe things weren't going to work out for almost anyone. It's even tempting to think that had we been in charge, if only God had consulted us, things could have gone differently. It looked very dark and dismal for those involved.

And into the darkness the greatest of lights shone brightly. How did that happen? It happened only through the relationships that these people had with God and with each other. Into the terrible conflict of Mary and Joseph came the light of trust and truth. Into the frightening darkness of unwed pregnancy came the light of a faithful fiat and, ultimately, the light of the Incarnation. Into the darkness of cousins meeting to share woman stories of pregnancy and confusion came the light of recognition and blessing. Mary, the unwed mother, and Elizabeth, the woman too old and tired to bear life, embraced and celebrated the life within each of them—life that would bring light and life to the world for endless ages! The song was born in their hearts: "The Mighty One has done great things for me, and holy is his name." The darkness of the whole mess was shattered as each person responded in total surrender to God's will and work in her or his life.

Can it be any different for us? Each of us has something to bring to birth. Each of us is confronted with impossible and improbable situations to accept or reject. Each of us has something to say "yes" to. Each of us is called to be recognized and to recognize others as bearers of Christ.

How important it is for us to be aware of and faithful to the John, the Joseph, the Mary, and the Elizabeth in each of us.

> **John:** Our mentor for evangelization, for humility, for knowing the truth, for keeping the focus where it belongs—on Jesus, the one who has come to save us.
>
> **Joseph:** Our mentor for accepting the brokenness and confusion born of thinking we know what's going on and having to trust completely in God and the people in our lives, and for entering fully and trustingly into relationships of love.
>
> **Mary:** Our mentor for believing that the likes of us can be the bearers of Christ, God-with-us, and for saying "yes" to improbable and impossible things—for believing that there is more to us than just us ourselves, for proclaiming that God who is the great one is doing great things in us.
>
> **Elizabeth:** Our mentor for discernment and recognition; for finding in the most unexpected places and persons the revelation and presence of God among us; for welcoming that revelation and presence into our lives; for allowing it to touch us, change us; for urging us to greet each other, regardless of circumstances, as the one who will bring the Christ to birth in our Church and in our world.

The Advent journey is our journey over and over again, day by day, year by year, for the rest of our lives. It is the journey of moving from the darkness into the light. It is the journey, too, of each member of our Church community who has been touched by the light and invited to proclaim it and celebrate it. The scriptures of Advent are rich. The practices and traditions—lighting the wreath, celebrating Posadas, collecting from our simple abundance to feed hungry people and bring smiles to the faces of poor children and their parents—all serve to encourage and support us on the journey. And most important of all is the willingness to embark again, always, today and tomorrow, on the journey with the faith that is born of our deepest longing. Longing for light, we wait in the darkness. And the light shines in the darkness.

PERSONAL REFLECTION
(30 minutes)

Invite the participants to reflect on and respond to the following questions in their journals:

- How are John the Baptist, Joseph, Mary, and Elizabeth models and mentors for me in my own faith journey? With whom do I most identify at this time in my life?

- What do John the Baptist, Joseph, Mary, and Elizabeth teach me about living out my baptismal commitment?

- What am I waiting for? How am I called to be an Advent person?

- What customs or practices would add richness to my personal experience of Advent? How will I live this Advent for others?

DIALOGUE
(30 minutes)

Invite the participants to share their journal entries with each other. Ask them to note any questions that emerge during their conversations in order to voice them later in the large-group discussion.

LARGE GROUP SHARING
(30 minutes)

Ask the participants to share their insights and questions with the large group. If there is time, facilitate a discussion of Advent practices such as the Advent wreath and Las Posadas. In parishes with diverse ethnic populations, invite people from various cultures to come and speak to the retreat group about their Advent and Christmas traditions.

CLOSING RITUAL
(30 minutes)

Gather once again in the church or chapel for the closing ritual, or provide a short break and change the ambience in the gathering space prior to celebrating the ritual. Add to the focal point a large lighted candle and provide tapers for each participant.

GATHERING SONG

Either a song focusing on the light of Christ or a setting of Psalm 27 is appropriate.

OPENING PRAYER

Presider *(with hands in the orans position)*:
God of Light, you have penetrated our darkness.
You reveal yourself to us.
May we, enlightened by your Holy Spirit, see you, hear you,
and touch you as you dwell among us.
We ask this in the name of Jesus, who is the Light of the World,
forever and ever.
Amen.

READING
1 John 1:1–5

INVITATION

Invite each participate to come forward and light a candle as she or he shares an Advent hope, dream, or action to be taken as a result of today's reflections and sharing.

RECOMMITMENT

Presider:

With a silent gesture, invite all to stand holding their lighted candles.

At our baptism, a covenant of unconditional love
was sealed between our God and each one of us.
We received the light of Christ into our hearts and were given a candle.
We were reminded to walk always as children of the light
and to keep the flame of faith alive in our hearts.
The Church prayed that when the Lord comes to meet each of us,
we would go out to meet him.
Go forth from this place, then, and wait for the Lord.
Prepare the way of the Lord.
Be ready when the Lord comes to you—
in silence, in the cries of your sisters and brothers,
in the darkness of a struggling world, in the surprises of each day.
Help one another, support one another, and pray for one another.
Go forth from this place and live an Advent life.
Go in peace.
All: Thanks be to God!

Pentecost Anniversary Retreat for the Fully Initiated

The Context

"On the anniversary of their baptism the neophytes should be brought together in order to give thanks to God, to share with one another their spiritual experiences, and to renew their commitment" (¶250 RCIA). This retreat is designed as an anniversary retreat to be held near or on the feast of Pentecost. The principal participants are the neophytes who have been fully initiated for at least a year. Those who have been initiated in recent years may also be invited. The retreat also is suitable for a parish community.

The purpose of this three-and-a-half-hour retreat is to reflect on the scriptures for the feast of Pentecost and to share experiences of living in faith as fully initiated members of the Church. It may be held on an evening as a twilight retreat, or on a weekend day.

The retreat includes a table gathering during which the neophytes share a meal and stories of their experiences as fully initiated members of the Church. It also offers them the opportunity to renew their baptismal commitment in a ritual at the conclusion of the retreat. The placement of the meal within the retreat schedule may be adjusted to accommodate the needs of the group and timing of the retreat. If possible, gather those who have been initiated during the past several years, particularly those who are completing the year of mystagogy. Their godparents, sponsors, and members of the parish community may join them. Ideally, the retreat would be held on an evening during the week prior to or just after the celebration of the feast of Pentecost.

Word of God

The scriptures of the feast of Pentecost form the basis for this retreat. The Reflection and Sharing is set in the context of the Liturgy of the Word. Acts 2:1–11 describes the coming of the Spirit as a mighty wind and tongues of fire to the gathered disciples. The responsorial psalm, Psalm 104, prays, "Lord, send out your Spirit and renew the face of the earth." 1 Corinthians 12 speaks of the many gifts of the Spirit given for the service of others. And John 20:19–23 proclaims that the gift of the Spirit is the peace of the risen Jesus that flows from compassion and forgiveness. A suggested homiletic presentation about gathering, service, and forgiveness is provided for the presider or retreat leader. It offers a framework within which to invite the neophytes to bring their lives to the Word and the Word to their lives, probing their experience as fully initiated members of the Church.

Pentecost is one of the few occasions when the Church adds the singing of a sequence to the Liturgy of the Word. This retreat is a wonderful occasion on which to call attention to this beautiful poetic prayer to the Holy Spirit that speaks in such strong images about the work of the Spirit in our daily lives.

According to the retreat design, the Liturgy of the Word is celebrated in full prior to the meal. Following the meal there is time for reflection and sharing. The retreat concludes with the renewal of baptismal promises.

SACRED SPACE

For this occasion, the table around which participants will gather to share their meal should be set in advance. If possible, provide tablecloths, flowers, candles, baskets of bread to be broken, wine glasses, and wine. The eucharistic imagery will add to the depth of the retreat experience.

You may wish to use the church or small chapel for the Liturgy of the Word and the concluding ritual. In the gathering space the focus should be on the place of proclamation, the Paschal candle or other large candle, and the font to be used for the renewal of baptismal promises. Renewing their baptismal commitment at the font used for their initiation will have special meaning for the participants.

If you are setting up a focal point in a gathering space or meeting room outside the church or chapel, create a font using a large bowl of water and set a branch for the sprinkling rite near the font. Provide tapers to be lighted at the renewal of promises for each participant. Using red fabric and candlelight will enhance the Pentecost theme. Let the liturgical symbols speak with noble simplicity and avoid cluttering the sacred space with other images such as doves, tongues of fire, or other common images of the Spirit.

LIVING RITE

This retreat is designed with ritual as the primary experience. The presider for the Liturgy of the Word should be well prepared, and comfortable using the postures and gestures appropriate to the presider's role.

In advance, work with music ministers to select musical versions of Psalm 104 and the sequence as well as the gathering and concluding songs.

You may wish to invite the pastor or other minister who presided at the initiation of the participants to preside at the Liturgy of the Word and/or at the concluding ritual. Making connections with their initiation experience will enhance the neophytes' experience of this gathering for renewal and recommitment.

GATHERING
(20 minutes)

Welcome the participants informally and, if appropriate, invite them to introduce themselves to one another. Encourage them to share briefly one of the following:

- Why they chose to come to this retreat
- A special memory from their initiation
- Something they have learned from the past year as fully initiated members of the Church.

This is not a time for discussion but an opportunity to connect with one another and to begin to create a sense of community among the participants.

LITURGY OF THE WORD
(40 minutes)

Following the order of worship for a Liturgy of the Word, celebrate the liturgy for the Mass during the Day on the feast of Pentecost, Year A. (If you choose to use the readings for the Vigil Mass, it will be necessary to prepare a homiletic reflection; the one provided here is based on the readings for Pentecost day.)

GATHERING SONG

GREETING

FIRST READING
Acts 2:1–11

RESPONSORIAL PSALM *(sung)*
Psalm 104

SECOND READING
1 Corinthians 12:3b–7, 12–13

SEQUENCE *(sung)*

GOSPEL ACCLAMATION *(sung)*

GOSPEL
John 20:19–23

HOMILETIC REFLECTION
(in these or similar words)
All powerful God, Father of our Lord Jesus Christ,
by water and the Holy Spirit
you freed your sons and daughters from sin
and gave them new life.
Send your Holy Spirit upon them
to be their helper and guide.
Give them a spirit of wisdom and understanding,
the spirit of right judgment and courage,
the spirit of knowledge and reverence.
Fill them with the spirit of wonder and awe in your presence.
(¶234 RCIA)

This prayer of the Church, this magnificent invocation, which you may remember from your own Rite of Confirmation, is a splendid summary of the Church's experience of and reflection upon the Pentecost event. This is the event that confirmed the very life and mission that Jesus shares with us through his own life, death, resurrection, and ascension to his Abba . . . and ours.

It is that same life and mission that has been entrusted to us, claimed as Christ's own through baptism. This is the life and mission that we have been hearing about throughout this Easter season—stories of courage and faith, stories of wonder and awe—as we reflect on the infant Church. Much like the realities of the present day, language, culture, and geography divided the early Christians, yet they pressed forward guided by the Spirit of the one they believed in and loved to death.

We as church pray with such boldness! We dare to pray, all the while knowing, naming, and expecting to receive God's very own Spirit! We do this because from generation to generation, God has revealed this same Holy Spirit in countless and marvelous ways, beginning at the time the Spirit hovered over the abyss in God's great creative moment. The Spirit's revelation continued throughout the ages to the moment when that same Spirit hovered over the waters of baptism as each of us, God's dearly beloved, was called by name to profess our faith and to die and rise with Christ.

Christ has died, Christ is risen, Christ has come and will come again and again and over and over again through the Holy Spirit, who was manifested and given to us when the time for Pentecost was fulfilled.

(The following is a creative, poetic reading meant to elicit a variety of images for further reflection.)

All in one place . . . gathered . . . Spirit . . . driving wind, fire and tongues and babble confusing babble . . . gifts different and many but one and varied . . . how? . . . tongues and languages . . . mighty acts of God . . . every nation under heaven . . . baptized as one and different kinds . . . one body and different gifts . . . one baptism all parts one body . . . all given to drink . . . many and one . . . all in one place . . . fear and locked . . . fear . . . rejoicing and gathered and peace . . . fear in their midst . . . breathed on them . . . peace . . . receive the Holy Spirit . . . forgive . . . breath . . . breathe . . . peace.

All the drama and profound imagery of the Pentecost event leads finally, simply, and deeply to the intimacy of relationship (what is more intimate than sharing breath?) and to peace.

How do we recognize the Spirit in our midst today? Where do we discover and live that intimacy and that peace? It may not be in driving winds and tongues of fire and apparitions from the dead. The mightiest acts of God may, in fact, be the simple, deep, and intimate acts the Church places before us in today's scriptures.

We recognize God's Spirit in our midst today when we *gather*, when we *serve*, and when we *forgive*.

❧ We recognize God's Spirit in our midst today . . . when we gather.

In all three of the Pentecost readings we find a strong sense of community. The community's gathering may be marked with fear, joy, proclamation, service, reconciliation. It may be a community gathered in homes or community centers, coffee shops or churches. But it is a community of real people living real lives believing in the real presence of the Lord in their midst.

Gathering is essential for us who believe. It is in our gathering that the intimacy of relationship is both celebrated and nurtured. It is in our gathering that our stories are told and understood. It is in our gathering that we celebrate the rhythm of the seasons and of our lives: the joy of birth, the grief of death, the marker moments and transitions, and plain old ordinary time. It is in our gathering that the variety of gifts and the mutual sharing of gifts for the sake of the mission of Jesus are recognized, supported, celebrated, and commissioned.

When we gather, with whom am I willing to gather? Who do I think shouldn't be there . . . and why? Do I separate the "okays" and the "not okays" in my heart? Have I determined who belongs and who the outsiders are? When we gather, do I come isolated or open, protective of or generous with my gifts? Do I gather into my heart and into our circle the suffering and the poor, the needy and the outcast, the stranger and the strange of the world whom our Abba wants to gather into one? What has gathering meant to me since my first time at the tables of God's Word and Eucharist?

- We recognize God's Spirit in our midst today . . . when we serve.

In all three of the Pentecost readings, we discover that the gifts given by the Spirit are not meant to be hoarded or hidden away. They are meant to be shared, spread around, and given away. At Pentecost, the gift of the Spirit burst forth in speech that was a proclamation of the mighty acts of God. This strange and wonderful gift wasn't about the people who could talk in some new and magical way. It was about God, whose mighty acts needed to be remembered in story, ritual, and prayer all over the world.

The ability to say, "Jesus is Lord" is not a gift of personal salvation or individualized redemption. Rather, it is a gift given in and through the community for the sake of the community. It is the foundation of many spiritual gifts that are all meant to be recognized and appreciated and put at the service of the one body. Sometimes that body is really broken and ugly, or smelly and sick, or drunk or abused. Sometimes I find that body in my way or in my face. Sometimes the body looks okay but is hurting and carrying secrets of pain and loneliness, fear and loss. The gifts given to each of us are not meant for the benefit of the gifted, but for the good of the body and the glory of God. So, what do I do with them?

The gifts of God's presence and peace are given for mission. We are sent forth with these gifts in Jesus' name. "As my Abba sent me, so I send you." And what I send you for is forgiveness, reconciliation, compassion, and healing. That's how you are to be in the world, in the world of your family and community, and in the world beyond your own. You are my disciples.

What are my gifts and where are they needed? What gifts do I need? What gifts am I called to bring forth in others?

- We recognize God's Spirit in our midst today . . . when we forgive.

What could be a more profound revelation of the Spirit in our midst than forgiveness and the resulting gift of peace? We hold in our hands and hearts the power to touch, to bless, to forgive, to bring peace—power given to us through the Holy Spirit.

Think of a time when you just knew you were forgiven (or when you were able to forgive) for being insensitive, thoughtless, or simply sinful. Allow yourself to remember that experience and what it feels like to know forgiveness and healing, understanding and gentle compassion, unconditional love and acceptance. And realize again the difference that it made in you and in those with whom you shared that reconciliation. That is the power that you have, I have, we have together as Church. What are we doing with this Pentecost power, the crown of all the gifts of the Spirit, the power to make peace?

To be forgiven and to forgive, to be loved and to love: this is the character of reconciliation that is at the heart of the mission that is ours as baptized, anointed ones. Reconciliation is what we celebrate each time we gather in the name of Jesus. Reconciliation is our mission as disciples sent forth to do as Jesus did.

To gather in the Spirit, to serve guided by the Spirit, and to forgive in the name of the Spirit—to be the manifestation and revelation of the Holy Spirit in our midst today, right here, right now, moment by moment—this is our Pentecost mission.

And so we pray . . .
All-powerful God, Abba of our Lord Jesus Christ,
by water and the Holy Spirit
you freed your sons and daughters from sin
and gave us new life.
Renew your Holy Spirit within us
to be our helper and guide.
Give us a spirit of wisdom and understanding,
the spirit of right judgment and courage,
the spirit of knowledge and reverence.
Fill us with the spirit of wonder and awe in your presence.

Invite the participants to be seated for a few moments of silent reflection.

INTERCESSIONS

If the group is not too large, invite spontaneous intercessions from the assembly. Otherwise, prepare intercessions in advance, prayers that reflect the reality of the times, the needs of Church and society, the cry of the poor, and the baptismal call to discipleship.

LORD'S PRAYER

SIGN OF PEACE

DISMISSAL

CONCLUDING SONG

TABLE GATHERING
(60 MINUTES)

Invite the participants to gather at table for a meal. No "grace" before meals is necessary; allow the movement from the table of the Word to give meaning to the gathering at the meal table.

REFLECTION AND SHARING
(20 minutes)

After the meal, return to the prayer space and invite the participants to remember the Liturgy of the Word. Ask:

- What do you remember?

- What particularly touched you?

- What word, phrase, or idea stays with you?

Invite them to share their responses with one other person.
Invite them to share something from their dialogue with their partner with the entire group.

JOURNAL REFLECTION
(20 minutes)

Distribute the journals. Invite the participants to respond to the questions in the journal. They should be encouraged to bring their experiences, questions, challenges, and insights from the past year(s) of living as fully initiated members of the Church.

all in one place
gathered
spirit
driving wind, fire and tongues and babble confusing babble
gifts different and many but one and varied
how?
tongues and languages
mighty acts of God
every nation under heaven
baptized as one and different kinds
one body and different gifts
one baptism all parts one body
all given to drink
many and one
all in one place
fear and locked
fear
rejoicing and gathered and peace
fear in their midst
breathed on them
peace
receive the Holy Spirit
forgive
breath
breathe
peace

We recognize God's Spirit in our midst today . . . when we gather.

- How has gathering with the worshiping assembly affected my life?
- What has gathering meant to me since my first time at the tables of God's Word and the Eucharist?
- What are the challenges and difficulties I have encountered in gathering for worship?

We recognize God's Spirit in our midst today . . . when we serve.

- What gifts have been given to me for the building up of the community?
- How have I given glory to God by putting my gifts at the service of others?
- What challenges or obstacles have I encountered in sharing the gifts I have been given?

We recognize God's Spirit in our midst today . . . when we forgive.

- Where and how have I experienced the Pentecost power to make peace?
- How have I experienced reconciliation and where do I need reconciliation with the Church?
- What questions, concerns, or needs for healing have I encountered as a fully initiated member of the Church?

GROUP SHARING
(30 minutes)

Invite the participants to gather in small groups to share their responses. Ask them to bring their questions, concerns, challenges, and difficulties to the large group. Invite a seasoned catechist or other resource person (this may be the retreat leader or presider) to facilitate the large-group session and to respond appropriately to the questions and issues that are raised.

At the end of the large-group session, invite the participants to renew their baptismal commitment with all the understanding that the past year has given them. Despite the challenges, questions, disillusionment, or obstacles of living as disciples, they are invited to recommit themselves to gospel values and participation in the life and mission of the Church as disciples of the risen Jesus.

RITUAL OF RENEWAL AND RECOMMITMENT
(20 minutes)

Gather around the baptismal font in the church or around the font that has been created in the gathering space.

GATHERING SONG
Choose an appropriate gathering song.

OPENING PRAYER
Leader:
Let us pray.
Open our ears, our hearts, and our minds, O God,
that we may hear your word
and be filled with your Holy Spirit.
We ask this through Christ, our Lord.
Amen.

With a gesture, invite the participants to be seated for the proclamation of scripture.

READING
ROMANS 6:3–11

DECLARATION OF INTENT
With a gesture, invite the participants to stand.

Leader:
Are you ready and willing to renew your baptismal promises and to recommit yourselves to a life of gospel values as disciples of Jesus Christ?

All respond.

Calling each person by name and taking time to listen to individual responses, ask:

Leader:
What do you ask of God as you renew your baptismal commitment today? And what do you ask of the Church?

As each person responds, invite her or him to light the taper from the paschal candle or large candle near the font.

When each of the participants (at least those who are completing the first year of mystagogy) has responded, continue in these words:

Leader:
My sisters and brothers, God uses the sacrament of water to give divine life to those who believe. Let us turn to God and ask that the gift of the Holy Spirit be renewed in us. May we be filled anew with the gift of life so that we may share it with strength and commitment as disciples of Christ.

Extending hands over the water, continue in these words adapted from the Rite of Baptism:

Leader:
Gracious God, you give us grace through sacramental signs,
which tell us of the wonders of your unseen power.
In baptism we use your gift of water,
which you have made a rich symbol of the grace
you give in this sacrament.

At the very dawn of creation,
your Spirit breathed upon the waters,
making them the wellspring of all holiness.
The waters of the great flood
you made a sign of the waters of baptism
that make an end of sin
and a new beginning of goodness in your Holy Spirit.
Through the waters of the Red Sea
you led Israel out of slavery
to be an image of your holy people,
set free from sin by baptism.

In the waters of the Jordan
your Son was baptized by John
and anointed with the Spirit.
Your Son willed that water and blood should flow from his side
as he hung upon the cross.
After his resurrection he told the disciples:
"Go, therefore, and make disciples of all nations,
baptizing them
in the name of the Father, and of the Son, and of the Holy Spirit."

Look now with love upon your Church gathered here today.
By the power of the Holy Spirit,
renew in us the grace of your Son,
which we received through our baptism.
May we who were buried with Christ in the death of baptism
rise also with him to newness of life.
May we be filled with your Holy Spirit.
We ask this through Christ, our Lord.
Amen.

Address those who will renew their baptismal promises in these or similar words:

Leader:
You have come here to renew your baptismal commitment. By water and the Holy Spirit, you have received the gift of new life from God, who is love.
We support you and encourage you and promise to walk with you so that, together, we may grow always stronger in faith and love.
Since your faith makes you ready, renew now the promises of your own baptism. Reject sin; profess your faith in Christ Jesus.

Using the ritual for the renewal of baptism, the presider leads the renewal of baptismal promises and the participants respond to each question saying, "I do."

Leader:
Do you believe in God, the Father almighty, Creator of heaven and earth?
Do you believe in Jesus Christ, God's only Son, our Lord, who was born of the Virgin Mary, was crucified, died, and was buried, rose from the dead, and is now seated at the right hand of the Father?
Do you believe in the Holy Spirit, the holy catholic Church, the communion of saints, the forgiveness of sins, the resurrection of the body, and the life everlasting?
This is our faith. This is the faith of the Church. May you always be proud to profess it in Christ Jesus, our Lord.

The presider invites the participants to come to the font to bless themselves with the waters of baptism. If this is not feasible, the presider sprinkles the gathered assembly with water from the font.

At the end of this water rite, indicate that the tapers should be extinguished. Conclude the ritual by inviting an exchange of the sign of peace with these or similar words:

Leader:
May we walk always as people of faith, children of light, messengers of the gospel, and disciples of Christ Jesus. Let us support and encourage one another through our prayer and witness. Let us offer each other a sign of peace.

The gathering may end informally as participants exchange the sign of peace and continue their conversations. Or, you may wish to select a concluding hymn to be sung before bidding the participants farewell.